LOST *at* WINDY CORNER

LOST _at_ WINDY CORNER

LESSONS FROM DENALI ON GOALS AND RISKS

by

AARON LINSDAU

Sastrugi Press

Jackson Hole, WY

Sastrugi Press / Published by arrangement with the author

Sastrugi Press: PO Box 1297, Jackson, WY 83001
www.sastrugipress.com

Lost at Windy Corner: Lessons From Denali On Goals and Risks

The author has made every effort to accurately recreate conversations, events, and lo-cales from his memories of them. To maintain anonymity, some names and details such as places of residence, physical characteristics, and occupations have been changed. The activities described in this book are inherently dangerous. The publisher does not have any control over and does not assume any responsibility for author or third-party websites or their content.

Any person participating in the activities described in this work is personally responsible for learning the proper techniques and using good judgment. You are re-sponsible for your own actions and decisions. The information contained in this work is subjective and based solely on opinions. No book can advise you to the hazards or anticipate the limitations of any reader. Participation in the described activities can result in severe injury or death. Neither the publisher nor the author assumes any lia-bility for anyone participating in the activities described in this work.

Library of Congress Control Number: 2014942992
Linsdau, Aaron
Lost at Windy Corner - 1st U.S. ed.
Summary: Aaron Linsdau sets out to climb Denali (Mt. McKinley) alone, a mountain notorious for dangerous weather, and challenges the reader to evaluate their own mea-sure of risk and reward.

ISBN-13: 978-1-64922-331-9 (paperback)

910.4

Printed in the United States of America
10 9 8 7 6 5 4 3 2

To Dad & Mom

*For nurturing my sense of adventure through
the Boy Scouts and for being there for me.*

TABLE OF CONTENTS

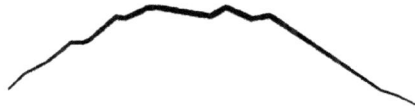

CHAPTER 1

Alaska

The landscape passed by on a highway that stretched to the horizon. Alfonso and I drove north on the Alaska Highway toward Talkeetna late into the evening. Even though it was 10:00 p.m. at night, the sun was still up. Both of us were bleary-eyed, as we had been traveling hard for several days straight. Our rental car smelled much older than it should, accentuating the feeling that we were taking a trip to somewhere wild and remote.

We were taking advantage of free flight vouchers we had received from Alaska Airlines after a problem flight earlier in the year. Had it not been for those tickets, we wouldn't now have been driving through the land of the midnight sun.

The route from Anchorage to Denali National Park follows a long, straight highway that rolls over gentle hills. For as far as the eye could see, an endless ocean of evergreens coated the landscape. Aside from a few roadside coffee stands, we had seen little other civilization since leaving Anchorage.

"How far is Denali?" asked Alfonso. "It feels like I've been driving forever."

"It can't be far now. The last sign I saw said forty miles," I replied. That was fifteen minutes ago.

"This is like one of those movies where the kids keep asking 'are we there yet?'"

"Agreed. I hope we find some place to sleep in Talkeetna. Otherwise, it's going to be a cold night in the car."

As we rolled up one particular hill, Alfonso became transfixed by something far ahead of us. Peering into the murky shadows, I saw a large moose wandering across the road. At first, I thought Alfonso was awestruck by the mammoth creature. He was born in Tijuana, Mexico and hadn't ever seen large wildlife outside of a zoo. I guessed it must be exciting for him to have such a sighting for the first time here in Alaska. Big animals can be mesmerizing. However, he wasn't slowing down. We were advancing on the bull moose at an uncomfortable clip.

"Hey, you might want to slow down for the moose," I said.

"What moose?" he asked.

"Uh, the huge moose up ahead in the road, dude."

"I don't see anything up ahead in the road."

We approached the point of no return where an animal strike became unavoidable. I pushed back in my seat. I couldn't understand why he wasn't slowing down. My skin prickled and my throat started to choke shut.

"Alfonso—moose. Just hit the brakes!" I yelled.

He and I had known each other for twenty years. We never yelled at each other. When either of us raised our voice, there was a serious problem. He did as I pleaded and slammed on the brakes. The anti-lock brakes chattered and the tires made an odd barking sound on the Alaskan asphalt. As we skidded to a halt, Alfonso came out of his daze.

"What the heck is that?" he asked.

"That's the moose I warned you about," I said.

"That's not a moose, that's a house on legs!"

I laughed out loud. His last-second braking had averted disaster. We were tired and hungry and we had nearly destroyed ourselves by driving into a 1,400-pound animal. Traveling on little sleep had resulted in another close call.

The moose stopped in the middle of the road. It turned its head and looked in our direction for a moment. Then, casually, he finished his walk across the road and disappeared into the forest.

"Are you really that tired? How did you not see that thing on the road?" I asked.

"I'm tired, but not that bad. I wasn't looking at the moose. I was looking at the insane mountain ahead."

"What do you mean? Those look no bigger than the foothills in San Diego to me."

"Are you kidding? That thing is huge."

"Sorry, what thing are you talking about?" I asked.

He glanced at me and saw the direction I was looking in.

"Oh, you're not looking high enough. Tilt your gaze up another twenty degrees."

I did as he asked. At first, I saw only clouds. Then, slowly, a shape materialized. It was so massive that my brain didn't register it for several seconds. At first, it looked like an oddly shaped cloud rather than a mountain. Then my brain latched onto what I was looking at. A huge massif stood out of the swampy Alaskan plain.

"What the…?" My voice trailed off.

"That's got to be Denali, right?" Alfonso asked.

"Honestly, I have no idea. I think it's something like twenty thousand feet high, but I'm not totally sure."

"That's what I was staring at while you were animal watching," he said.

"Good thing I was, otherwise we'd be chewing on moose hide and windshield glass."

The mountain was so high that the peak was invisible as we drove downhill. Alfonso decided to pull over to the side of the road. There was little traffic on the Denali Highway. We wanted to stop and get a better look at the thing.

"I can't believe how big it is," Alfonso told me. "It makes the mountains back home look like molehills."

"Yeah. Well, I'm betting that has to be Denali. But we'll ask someone when we reach Talkeetna."

We gathered our wits and hopped back in the car. After driving for another forty-five minutes, we reached the Alaskan hamlet of Talkeetna. We immediately discovered one of the realities about Alaskan travel. Showing up in a town and hoping to find lodging at midnight is a mistake. It took half an hour of looking around to find nearly everything booked. The only place with room wanted $150 for the night. We had scheduled our bus ride into Denali National Park for 8:00 a.m. It was the first ride in. We had to leave Talkeetna at 5:00 a.m. to make it to the park in time.

"There's no way I'm spending that kind of money to sleep for five hours," Alfonso said. "Plus the place looks pretty sketchy."

"You're right. Let's just find a place to park and sleep in the car. It'll suck but that's just way too much money."

Alfonso drove us to an empty dirt lot and parked the car facing Denali.

"Did that clerk really say that we were lucky to have seen the mountain?" I asked.

"Yah, you heard right. She said it's visible only every third day on a good week. So we were lucky."

"I wonder what it would be like to climb that thing. Isn't it one of the seven summits?"

"I think so. It's the highest mountain in North America, if my geographic memory serves me right."

I stared up at the peak. "If it's clouded in that often, it must be a beast to climb."

"It would certainly be a lot different to the sport climbing we do on the weekends. Those lenticular clouds above it mean high winds, usually above fifty miles per hour."

"Being up there in a raging storm must make things pretty exciting."

"Ha, ha. I think we'll leave that for another time. We'd better get sleep or we're going to be totally wasted for tomorrow."

"Sounds good. I'm already wasted. We'll probably regret sleeping in this little Corolla."

"I'm sure we will. That's the cost of being poor."

Alfonso and I used our jackets as blankets and did our best to sleep. The humidity forced us to roll the windows down. That, in turn, let the cold air in. It was an unpleasant night. As I drifted in and out of sleep, I kept peeking at Denali through heavy eyelids.

"I sure would like to try climbing that mountain some day," I murmured.

"I'm sure you do. I'd rather sleep now. Let's think about it more tomorrow," said Alfonso.

We had plenty of time to discuss climbing Denali as we explored Alaska during that August week in 2004.

Denali seen from the Anchorage to Talkeetna highway.

Chapter 2

Final Training
May 1, 2016

Loaded with a fifty-pound pack, ankle weights, and razor-sharp crampons, I crunched my way through the snow up Glory Mountain. My goal was to keep my climb time under an hour. Training on this 10,000-foot mountain improved my strength and confidence, both of which I would need on my upcoming expedition.

The sky was gray and overcast. A gentle snow fell, coating my jacket with a crispy shell of ice. As I walked the last ramp of snow and crested the peak, a cold blast of air cut across my face. Snow started driving into my eyes. I pulled down my goggles to halt the stinging. A few skiers took sidelong glances at my oversized backpack.

I smiled and looked around. The entire Teton mountain range was invisible. In fact, I couldn't see more than a few hundred feet away. The wind rustled my hood, filling my ears with the sound of flapping nylon.

These were the perfect training conditions for my imminent Denali climb. The tougher the weather, the better. I had committed myself to climbing the highest peak in North America only five months before. After researching, reading, and speaking to others about climbing Denali, formerly known as Mt. McKinley, I knew it was going to be difficult. It even had the potential to be lethal. Many climbers have perished on Denali's slopes. I was training so that I too didn't become a statistic. That's why I was on the top of Glory Mountain in a storm.

As I made my way down the trail, I passed skiers marching uphill. The snow piled up fast. It filled in their boot tracks almost as quickly as they were made. With the heavy pack and ankle weights, I had to be careful. Though the slope wasn't steep, a stumble would send me sliding into rocks and trees.

On the steepest part of the climb down, I paused to consider the way ahead. The next section was only ten feet long, but tricky. Should I snag a crampon, I would take a headlong dive down the hill. To secure myself, I buried the pick of my ice axe into the slope, before taking my first step, and then another. All went well. As I flexed my arm to pluck the axe out of the ice, however, the snow under my boots suddenly crumbled and the path of snow holes I was following disappeared in a miniature avalanche. The entire face gave way beneath me, tumbling downward. My body slammed into the slope and I hung in mid-air, prevented from falling only by my grip on the axe.

My right arm was outstretched in an awkward Superman pose, pointing toward the summit. The red half-inch nylon strap squeezed my wrist, squashing my glove's insulation, but held firm. In a few moments, I regained my composure and tried to figure out what to do next. The bones in my wrist pinched, sending electric shocks up my fingers. I made a fist to grip the Black Diamond Raven Pro ice axe handle to relieve the pressure.

After working out for four months, I should have been able to pull myself up with one arm and kick new footholds. Unfortunately, my Gregory expedition pack, loaded with four gallons of water and a fifty-meter climbing rope, made a one-armed pull-up impossible. For the same reason, I couldn't push myself away from the ice wall to regain my footing. The ankle weights made it feel like someone was tugging my boots, trying to drag me down the slope.

Although my ice axe was buried deep in the snow, I knew the 230 pounds of me and my pack might easily break it loose, sending me tumbling. It occurred to me that the whole scenario probably looked like something from a bad mountain climbing movie, where the main character flails about desperately trying to regain a foothold. I tried not to panic.

First I tried to kick the front points of the crampons into the snow face. The crampons only found loose snow and gained no purchase. Every time I kicked, I felt the ice axe twist back and forth.

I was running out of time. My fingers grew cold from the pressure. Who knew how long the ice axe would hold? To regain a foothold, I needed to push my body outwards and bury my legs in the slope. The backpack and soft snow made pushing out with my left hand impossible; my arm sank to the elbow and I twisted sideways.

The only way to regain my footing was to throw my body away from the slope, then kick in as I was in the air. Doing this would likely pry the axe from its hold, the only thing preventing me from falling. Calmly, I breathed in and out. Then I threw my whole weight out from the slope and, while in the air, pointed my legs toward the mountain. I buried both boots and regained my footing.

As I recovered, I laughed out loud. People climb and ski this slope all day, yet here I was, the only person in danger, while on the way down. I had nearly crashed into a tangle of trees and rocks. It wouldn't have been a very long fall, but far enough to injure someone with a backpack. Most anyone who has climbed this route might laugh at the predicament I got myself into. They might think it was impossible to fall and be injured in a micro-avalanche like that. Yet, there I was.

Had I lost my hold with the axe, I might have flipped over, tumbling head-first into a boulder. Or I might have been skewered by a broken branch. Less likely, I could have landed in a soft pile of snow and been just fine.

It was a perfect training moment. The threat of injury was real. I might find myself dangling from an ice axe with a full pack high on Denali, but now I knew how to rescue myself and how fast I needed to act. I hoped I would not need my new knowledge.

That was the toughest moment of my full summit training day. After the mini-avalanche, the rest of the descent went without incident. Once I reached the road on Teton Pass, at 8,431 feet, I still had another two hours of hiking. Instead of driving up and parking on the pass, I had started the climb far below. My final destination was a parking lot another 2,000 feet lower along the Old Pass Road.

In order to simulate the grueling experience of climbing Denali, I had loaded a sled with a sixty-pound bag of sand and dragged it up from the base of the mountain. This was in addition to my fifty-pound pack and ankle weights. This sled and pack weight was a real simulation for the food, fuel, and gear I would be hauling in Alaska in a few weeks.

Once I returned to my sled, I strapped on my MSR Lightning Ascent snowshoes, clipped the sled to my backpack with Black Diamond carabiners, and began walking down. When I had started climbing in the morning, the snow was solid from the cold night before. Halfway up, the sun came out and turned the snow to slush. Dragging the sled with snowshoes that sank four inches each step had turned into a thigh-burning affair.

Now, tramping downhill, I faced another challenge. The sled kept slipping down the slope and slamming into my legs, repeatedly knocking me over. It was another good simulation of the Denali experience to come.

From my Yellowstone expeditions, I had learned a trick to slow the sled down by tying several feet of rope under the bottom of the sled. These snagged on the snow, increasing drag. The sled now stuttered along, maintaining its position.

By the time I reached my truck, the sun had long since set. The temperature had plummeted, forcing me to don my Eddie Bauer down parka, then risen till I was overheating and then dropped back to freezing. For half an hour it had even risen high enough to produce rain. I relished the tough conditions, however. I knew that Denali would throw this and more at me.

~

The three components needed to build yourself and increase your value to others are: a commitment to better yourself (courage), a desire to face whatever challenge you're presented with (grit), and the ability to remain cheerful while focusing on your goal, regardless of the problems that crop up (attitude).

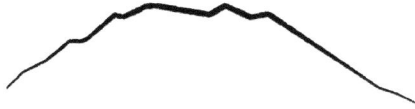

CHAPTER 3

From Jackson to Talkeetna

As I walked up to the security checkpoint at the Jackson Hole Airport, I felt like I had brought too much. My Kelty Redwing backpack was overloaded to the point of bursting. I carried my Millet Everest climbing boots in a separate handbag. With all my jackets on, I looked like the Michelin Man waddling through security.

The reason I carried my most important gear was to avoid the risk of lost baggage. If, for some reason, the airline or one of the airports lost my boots, I would be unable to replace them in Anchorage. It's not uncommon for expeditions to have their bags delayed, whether they are misplaced, lost, or misdirected. When I'm on an expedition, every piece of gear matters to me. If I could somehow compress everything into a single small backpack, I would.

One of the challenges of this trip was the fact that there were three short flight connections. Should anything go wrong with one, I would miss the others. Should that happen, it was impossible to guess where my sled, food, and tent would end up. Flying out of a mountain town is fraught with potential hazards, such as poor weather, which might cause a flight cancellation.

The first two connections, in Salt Lake and Seattle, went well. I had exactly enough time to walk off one plane and onto another. My third flight connection wasn't as smooth. The flight attendants shut the door for our Seattle to Anchorage flight as normal. And then we sat. And we sat some more. Finally, the captain came on the intercom.

"Sorry, folks. We've had a mechanical issue develop with the plane. We're having maintenance look at it and will update you as soon as we know something."

Groans rippled up and down the aircraft.

At least this was the last leg of my flight, so a delay wouldn't cause me to miss another flight. The inability to call my shuttle from Anchorage to Talkeetna was a problem, however. Other people were booked on my Alaskan ride. If I didn't arrive on time, I wasn't sure what would happen.

After nearly an hour, the Delta Airlines mechanics worked their magic. The plane was pronounced airworthy once more and we were off. There was nothing I could do about my shuttle, so I settled into my seat for the four-hour flight to the Last Frontier state.

As soon as I arrived, I called Gary at Go Purple Shuttle and let him know I had arrived. He didn't answer. I contemplated the rotating baggage carousel and sighed. It looked like I'd missed my ride. My one consolation was that all of my bags eventually disgorged themselves out of the bowels of the Ted Stevens airport.

After fifteen minutes, I received a call from Gary.

"Where are you? We didn't hear anything," he said.

"I'm sorry about that. My flight to Anchorage was delayed."

"We're not too far out of the city, so we can turn around and pick you up."

"Wow! Thank you so much. Sorry for the inconvenience. If I had my own private plane, I would've been here on time."

"If you had your own private plane, you wouldn't need a shuttle driver," Gary replied.

I laughed out loud. A few people at the baggage carousel glanced over at me, and then went back to their phones.

"Good point. I'll be outside waiting."

"Okay, see you shortly."

The phone clicked off. I felt truly blessed to have a driver and passengers willing to return and pick me up. My briefing with the Denali National Park climbing rangers was tomorrow. If I missed the appointment, I wasn't sure how long this would delay my expedition.

As promised, Gary drove up fifteen minutes later. He packed me into his passenger van, which was full of climbers.

"Hey, guys, sorry about the delay. My Seattle flight nearly didn't happen."

Bill Bradley, an extreme endurance athlete and the oldest climber in the van, grinned. "No problem. My flight was delayed, too. Gary fixed us all up."

"Well, thank you for coming back to get me, Gary."

"That's okay. We'll make our way to Talkeetna with plenty of light."

The three younger climbers in the back asked me who I was climbing with.

"No one," I answered.

"But you have a company you're climbing with, right?" one of them asked.

"Nope, I'm going solo on this one. I skied alone to the South Pole a few years ago, so I'm comfortable with crazy solo travel."

"That's nuts!"

It was May in Alaska. The sun wouldn't set until after 10:30 p.m. All of the climbers in the van were relying upon the never-dark sky to successfully climb Denali. Even in the early hours of the morning there would still be enough light to make a summit bid.

To break up the two-hour drive from Anchorage to Talkeetna, Gary stopped at a small shack alongside the highway. It was a water, coffee, and bathroom break for everyone. He also bought everyone a homemade peanut butter cookie.

"These are the best peanut butter cookies you will ever have in your life. Welcome to Alaska," he chimed as he passed the treats around.

A chorus of thank yous rang out in the white Ford passenger van.

Though I don't normally enjoy peanut butter cookies, this one was delectable. I wondered if it was the anticipation of living off bars and freeze-dried food that made it taste so good. Whatever the case, I savored it like it was my last meal.

Gary asked everyone what company everyone was flying with. I was the only one not flying with Talkeetna Air Taxi (TAT).

"Why did you go with K2?" Gary asked.

Roadside Alaskan refreshments.

"I saw that Bradford Washburn had flown with them a few years ago," I replied. He established the West Buttress Route, the most popular path up Denali. "I thought he might know something. That, or he had a hook-up."

"TAT are always the first to take off, and then everyone else follows," Gary said.

"That's interesting. Did I make a mistake?" I asked.

"Oh, no, not at all. I just like to collect information on why someone would take another company besides TAT, because they're the ones with the best weather forecasting. They fly the most up there."

The short conversation gave me something to brood about for the rest of the drive to Talkeetna. Though all of the Denali flight companies appeared to offer the same service, only K2 Aviation had called me after my email inquiry. They were proactive, so I gave them my business. It seemed that other companies, apart from K2 and TAT, rarely flew climbers to the mountain, though their websites suggested otherwise.

When we arrived in Talkeetna, the clouds hung low and the sky threatened rain. Gary helped me unload my gear at the K2 hangar. I shook his hand and thanked him for returning to the airport to collect me.

"It was my pleasure. I make sure everyone gets to where they need to be."

"When should I call you for a pick-up after my climb?"

"Any time."

"I'll make sure not to wake you up. My flight is really early."

"No, seriously," he countered. "I'll pick up groups even in the middle of the night. I answer the phone twenty-four hours a day."

"Good to know. I'm glad to have someone I can rely on."

"Have a safe climb. I'll see you when you get back!"

Gary hopped into the van and drove off. Like every other solo trip, I now stood truly alone at the beginning of the adventure. There was no one to greet me or provide directions. After sleuthing around, I found the K2 Aviation office.

Walking in, I found the place abuzz with activity. The front desk clerk said the weather had been bad for days. Climbers were experiencing the "Talkeetna Hang"—that is, they were stuck until flights could resume. That meant climbers on the mountain were equally stuck. It was a good reminder that I had to be flexible.

"Welcome to Alaska," she said.

"Where's a good place to camp?" I asked.

"You're not really supposed to camp on the airport lawn anymore. The town cracked down on that."

I asked if the young man at the counter could call around and find a place for me to stay. He picked up the phone and dialed without consulting a phone book or list. After a few short words, he hung up.

"There's room at Latitude 62," he said.

"Why did you choose that place?" I asked.

"Because my mom works there."

I laughed. "Welcome to small-town Alaska."

The hotel was a few hundred yards from the hangar, across the railroad tracks. I had to make two trips to haul my 130 pounds of gear. I felt like a sherpa carrying the massive sled on my back. Though I was strong from training, I hadn't practiced carrying a loaded sled on my back. My progress was halting but I finally dragged everything over. I needed to prepare for a possible flight tomorrow and I wanted to arrange my gear in the comfort of a room rather than in the hangar, where I might lose something.

Latitude 62 was the quintessential Alaskan hotel. Each room had a heater and blackout curtains to keep the midnight sun at bay. The hallway connected to a bar and restaurant. It was a one-stop-shop experience.

After preparing my gear, I walked into town for lunch. I found a food trailer situated outside of the Frontier Gifts shop. A menu scrawled on a whiteboard offered a three-quarter pound pulled pork sandwich. I knew I wouldn't have proper food for weeks, so that's what I ordered. The pile of meat was fantastic. Bob, the man running the trailer, loaded me up with all the sauce I could stand. He had a classic Alaskan runaway story.

"I moved to Alaska because I lost my son a bit back," he said.

"Sorry to hear that, Bob. I can't image what you went through as a parent."

"It was tough. Life went downhill pretty quick. I went into a dark place and knew I was in trouble. I needed a major change. So I sold everything, packed what I had in two duffles, and showed up in Talkeetna."

"Just like that?"

"I couldn't stand going to all the places I went to with my son. Everywhere in Buffalo, New York reminded me of him."

"You went from one cold place to another."

"It's not too bad. I kept this memento of my time together with my boy."

Bob pulled out a polished necklace pendant made from a rifle shell. It glittered in the fading sunlight.

"Did you two go shooting a lot?"

"All the time. He was really good. I taught him everything I knew."

"Bob, remember this," I told him. "Although your son isn't with you anymore, he's not gone. As long as you remember and hold him in your heart, he'll be with you."

Bob looked down at the counter for a moment. Then he nodded.

"I know it's not the same as actually having him around," I conceded, "but if you share stories about him, like you have with me, he'll live on."

"Yah, that's true. Maybe I'll write a book about our time together," Bob said.

"That'd be a nice touch. Put together some stories and make it tug at the heart. Email me when you have something. I know a publisher."

"That's great. Thanks. Well, I better get back to work here. Don't want to be fired from my new job."

I smiled at Bob and gave him a fist bump rather than a shake of the hand as he handled food and wanted to keep things as sanitary as possible.

I hoped the Alaskan gifts in the Frontier Gifts shop would prove different to those in my hometown of Jackson Hole. They weren't. But at least the staff had excellent stories.

Laura, the owner, told me about her midnight encounter with a stranger in Alaska. She explained that she and her husband ran a small bed-and-breakfast outside of Talkeetna. One evening, near midnight, she saw a car drive up the road and park in front of the house.

She looked out the window suspiciously. No guests were expected. Their place was difficult to find and people never showed up unannounced. As she looked out the curtains, she saw a man step out of the car. He gripped a baseball bat in his hand. As he walked up the porch, Laura opened the door to greet him.

In her hands she held a Mossbarger 500 Home Defense 12-gauge shotgun.

"I raised the gun and asked my visitor if I could help him. He stared in shock for a moment, then dropped the bat and ran to his car. I was impressed how fast he moved," she drawled in her Texas accent.

"Does everyone here carry?" I asked.

"You better believe it. I have my .44 right here." She patted her hip. "Never know when you'll run into a grizzly while picking berries."

"So he got away?"

"Not quite. I gave him a farewell reminder. I peppered his trunk with buckshot."

I chuckled. "Did you call the cops?"

"Sure, but the next day. I didn't want to wake the local sheriff up. He lives sixty miles away. You have to be self-sufficient here."

"Did you get a license plate or anything?"

"No, but I didn't need to. The trooper was mad that I didn't call him that night. But he knew to keep an eye out for a car with a shot-up rear."

"You Alaskans sure are entertaining. There always seems to be something going on somewhere in this huge state. You move up from Texas?"

"Sure did. My husband and I got tired of the heat and wanted something different. Our daughter hated it at first. Now she swears she'll never leave."

"Kids are funny that way."

We chatted a bit more before I bought gifts for my family and took my leave. I reveled in all the different characters I met in Talkeetna. It took all of five minutes to walk across town, so everyone knew each other.

To finish the day I enjoyed a reindeer steak at the town's brewpub, which was packed with climbers sharing stories over beer. I slept fitfully, however. Resting well before an expedition can be difficult, though I did my best to get my head down. I knew that if K2 flew tomorrow, my first day would be very long.

~

The effort of reaching the starting line can provide valuable lessons. You never know what you might learn from unexpected people you meet along the way.

CHAPTER 4

May 10
Green trees to white glacier

No matter how much time I have before catching an expedition flight, I never sleep well. I end up awake early, waiting for the alarm clock to sound. The excitement of playing out a hundred scenarios thunders through my mind, making sleep fleeting.

Have I prepared enough for this expedition? What if, what if? No matter how many times I do this, the excitement and stress results in a poor night's sleep. I have never figured out a technique to keep my brain calm before an expedition.

After enjoying a six-dollar breakfast of sausage and biscuits, I checked out of the hotel, grabbed my climbing permit paperwork, and walked out of Latitude 62. I headed for the Denali national park ranger station. The walk across Talkeetna took less than fifteen minutes. The town is small and has no stoplights and only a few stop signs.

I arrived at the ranger station a few minutes before my appointment time. This allowed me time to review this season's climbing statistics. The information board didn't paint a picture of climbing success. None of the eighteen climbing attempts thus far had been successful.

From what I understood of Denali, the idea was that the earlier one climbed in the season, the more stable the weather was. The park statistics board painted an entirely different picture. There was no data from the early season last year to compare against. All I knew now was that I faced a tough challenge as a solo climber.

Current mountain climbing information.

At 8:30 a.m., climbing ranger Frank summoned me into the conference room to discuss my upcoming trek. All Denali climbers are required to attend the briefing, regardless of experience or number of times on the mountain. As I was climbing solo, I expected an earful of advice and admonitions to discourage me from the attempt.

"Ready to go over the climbing presentation?" he asked.

"Sure am. Let's get this started so I can catch my flight," I replied.

"Okay, let's see what you've done thus far," he said.

Frank read over my application paperwork. In it was the required supplemental solo form detailing my plans and experience. He surveyed the sheet for a few moments.

"Wow!" he exclaimed.

"I'll bet you don't get a lot of those?" I asked.

"No, for sure."

"I'm curious. Have you met many solo polar explorers?"

"Nope, you're the first one I've ever met."

"Actually, I'm surprised."

"No, tons of Himalayan climbers, other ranges, but none soloing to the SP."

"I hope I gave you a pleasant surprise, then."

"Quite. Let's get to the slideshow."

Frank seemed to dispense with some of the usual discussions about the slides he must have with other solo climbers. I wasn't sure, though. He was a total professional. It just felt as though he breezed through the technicalities of the climb without bothering with any rookie admonitions. He warned me about the common crevasse locations, where to dispose of poop bags, and how to manage emergency communications.

This was my first Denali briefing. I was happy that he didn't give me a lecture about being cautious, that I really shouldn't be on the mountain by myself. I knew the park couldn't deny me the permit. My assumption was that they would dissuade solo climbers based on experience.

At the end of the presentation, Frank handed me a CMC (Clean Mountain Can, a poop can) with only a lid strap. I asked him if he could provide me a can with a set of carrying straps.

"Sure thing, let me go find one for you."

I was amazed how responsive and friendly he was. Frank excused himself and went to find me a fully kitted can. In what seemed an instant, Frank returned. He proudly carried a fully strapped CMC. My interviews with other rangers on my solo expeditions have been professional but brusque. This was a welcome relief.

"There you go. Are there any other questions you have?"

"Nope, thanks for your time. You've been great and a real pro."

"Thank you! That's my goal here. Have a good climb."

I shook Frank's hand and left him to prepare for the next group of climbers, who were waiting eagerly in the lobby for their appointment in the station's climbing history room. As they filed in, I took the opportunity to examine the collection of Denali artifacts.

At the entrance to the room was a three-ring binder containing the collected climbing history of Denali. I found some interesting statistics in it, among them the number of successes, failures, and records set on the mountain. Killian Jornet's name stood out—he climbed the mountain in a mere eleven hours forty-eight minutes. I noted that he did a complete acclimation climb prior to setting this stunning record. It would take me longer to climb to the summit and back from 14,000 feet than he took for his entire round trip—and he began at base camp, from the aircraft ice strip on Kahiltna Glacier. That meant a round trip of nearly thirty miles with over 13,000 feet of elevation gain.

Was his training regimen that superior? Did he have ultra-athlete genetics, beyond those of the normal human? Or was it a combination of both?

1992	1,070	555	515	48
1993	1,108	438	670	60
1994	1,277	575	702	55
1995	1,220	697	523	43
1996	1,148	659	489	43
1997	1,110	548	561	51
1998	1,166	746	420	36
1999	1,183	675	508	43
2000	1,209	579	630	52
2001	1,305	533	772	59
2002	1,232	587	645	52
2003	1,179	489	688	58
2004	1,275	619	656	51
2005	1,340	565	775	58
2006	1,152	571	581	50
2007	1,218	645	573	47
2008	1,272	517	755	59
2009	1,161	479	682	59
2010	1,222	552	670	55
2011	1,232	545	687	56
2012	1,223	725	498	41
2013	1,151	346	787	68
2014	1,204	775	429	36
2015	1,092	464	628	58
Totals:	41,976	20,049	21,906	52%

Previous year climbing information.

I thought that if it was purely training, I could follow his program. Then I might accomplish a similar future feat with my forty-two-year-old body. But if his genes were responsible, I had no hope. My history of childhood asthma always stymied any athletic achievements. No matter how much I trained, I still had trouble dropping my time for the mile to seven minutes.

What I have learned about myself is that I climb slowly. I can grind out distance and drive my body to the point of falling asleep while riding a bicycle. Even though I had trained hard for Denali, carrying heavy backpacks with ankle weights up mountains, I never felt like it was enough. My climbing speed had steadily improved throughout the spring, but I never felt like I could jog up the mountain.

Examining the logbook planted the seed of doubt in my mind. The "what-ifs" started marching through my mind. What if I fell in a crevasse? What if I was trapped at high camp for a week and my supplies failed? What if I was injured and couldn't call for rescue. Being a solo climber means having mental struggle as a constant companion. But I knew there would be many other climbers on the mountain to chat with.

Teams can keep individuals going long after they would have quit by themselves. That's what makes solo exploration so difficult. There's no one to rely on when something goes wrong. The only source of energy a solo climber has to draw from is within. That's why I have trained myself to obey the orders of a mental drill sergeant with the voice of Ronald Lee Ermey from the movie *Full Metal Jacket*.

Shaking my head, I collected myself. It was pointless to think negatively about the future. All I could do was to climb safely and have faith that it would all work out. My mind returned to the room I was in and I continued my tour.

At the end of the room was a stone fireplace made out of rounded river rock. An array of boots sat on the hearth. This collection of climbing boots spanned everything from modern to seemingly ancient. On one side was a pair of yellow plastic double climbing boots that looked similar to a downhill ski boot. On the other side, dating back to the beginning of climbing as a sport, was a dingy brown leather boot. It sported hobnails punched into the sole for grip. How many toes had been lost after climbing with boots like those?

Historic Denali climbing boots, old to modern, left to right.

Thoughts of food invaded my mind as I walked across Talkeetna after leaving the ranger station. I desperately wanted to enjoy a last big meal. First I had to stop at K2 Aviation to show them my completed climbing permit. Without it, they would not fly me to the mountain. I didn't want to miss a flight window because I had stopped for lunch. If nothing else, I could munch on my first day's rations before flying.

The office was as busy as before. It seemed like there was never a calm moment in there. After showing the desk clerk my park permit, I paid the final balance for my flight.

Sorry, we can't take off right now. The weather has closed in on the glacier.

My spirits dropped.

"I heard planes taking off earlier in the morning. Did this just move in?"

"Yes, don't worry. It's totally normal. We call it the Talkeetna Hang."

"So I might have time for lunch."

"You sure do. Give us your number and we'll call you when the weather clears."

She wrote down my number on a yellow legal pad.

"Should I just stop by again after lunch?"

"Yes, but don't worry, we'll call you if we're flying."

They had me place all of my gear in a locked Quonset hut. It would remain there until I returned. I carefully laid it all out as I didn't want anything to get missed if we left in a rush. Every expedition starts with a period of boredom that eventually ends in panicky haste.

Walking onto K2's patio deck, I felt dejected. If only I had scheduled my ranger appointment for the day before I'd be on the mountain at this very moment. Then I realized how silly such feelings were. Predicting a weather window five months in advance was impossible. It seemed the mountain changed from hour to hour, with no guarantees.

"Have confidence," I told myself. "At least you can grab a real bite to eat."

And that I did.

Walking across the train tracks to the outskirts of Talkeetna, I had the perfect lunch in mind. I set my sights on the trailer where Bob served up those mountains of meat. Thoughts of a three-quarter pound pulled pork sandwich made me salivate. I quickened my pace.

After powering down the whole meal of meat, bun, black beans, coleslaw, and an orange Fanta soda, I basked in the warm sunlight. The air was still cool from the rainstorm last night and a light breeze rippled the park bench umbrella. I thanked Bob for his cooking.

"You're welcome. Good luck and be safe on the mountain."

"You betcha. I need to return in one piece. I have things to do," I replied.

Dumping the remains of my meal in the gray trashcan, I strolled back to the K2 hangar to see what was going on. I discovered my sled and backpack were nowhere to be seen. Only my body-sized blue duffle remained.

My first thought was, "Oh great, who stole all of my gear?" Then, looking around, I realized all the other climbing gear was missing from the hangar. The moment of shock subsided and I looked toward the airfield. On the tarmac, several climbers, complete with their gear, surrounded a single engine Otter aircraft.

That was my flight!

Single engine Otter used to ferry climbers to the Kahiltna glacier.

I checked my iPhone 6 for a missed call. Nothing. No texts, either. For a moment, I was more than a little irritated.

"They were supposed to call me," I muttered to myself as I jogged over to the aircraft.

My climbing gear was waiting next to the plane. Excitement replaced annoyance and I forgot about the non-existent phone call.

Walking past the other climbers, I asked if this was my flight.

Michael, the pilot, confirmed it was. "Yes, we're headed to the glacier. The weather cleared and we have a chance to fly up there."

Michael was a tall and confident-looking man, with aviator glasses and closely cropped haircut. As he focused on rotating the propeller, inspecting each blade in turn, he told me I needed to hurry.

"We had better take off as soon as possible. If the weather closes in again, it might ground flights for the rest of the day."

"Okay, let me drop my stuff in the office and I'll be right out," I said.

It was good I didn't dawdle while at lunch. My gear would have flown to the mountain without me—and I had no idea what would have been done with it once on the glacier.

Rushing into the office, I asked to have my phone, charger, keys, and wallet locked up. None of them would be useful on the mountain so there was no reason to carry the extra weight or have to worry about losing them.

"I didn't get a call about the flight."

"Sorry, we've been a little busy with shuttling climbers back and forth."

"Alright. If you don't mind, I need to drop my street clothes into the locker so I can board my flight."

The clerk took me to the Quonset hut and unlocked it. After I had slipped on my Millet climbing boots, I clomped heavily about on the plywood floor. The boots were perfect for glacier travel but awkward for dancing around piles of equipment.

Thanking the clerk, I waddled over to the airplane. I couldn't help smiling at the building excitement I felt at flying to Denali in this small aircraft.

I was the last to clamber up the steel ladder with its chipped red paint. Taking my seat, I put on the ear protection, which had a microphone attached. After clattering the ladder into the airplane, Michael hopped in and locked the door. Walking down the short aisle, he made sure that everyone was buckled in.

All of the equipment and climbers were onboard. Michael finished his inspection and began on his preflight checklist. He walked back through the aircraft, jiggling the rear door handle and double-checking everything. After he had ensured the plane was airworthy, he addressed the five other climbers and me.

"Hello, everyone. Welcome to your flight up to Denali K2 Aviation. We'll be flying in this single-engine Otter to the Kahiltna Glacier."

Everyone was paying rapt attention.

"Once we arrive there, I ask that everyone help with unloading the aircraft. The weather is unstable and we need to turn this around quickly."

One couple spoke no English, so another climber quietly translated for them. Michael covered the safety features, focusing especially upon the location of the fire extinguisher and the emergency transponder.

"Hopefully we won't need to figure out how to work that thing," one of my fellow-passengers joked.

"No, you shouldn't need to," Michael answered. "But, this is the Alaska Range."

No one added any more remarks. The point was well taken. The skies were clear now, but violent weather can whip up almost instantly in these high Alaskan mountains. A little bit of knowledge could make all the difference in a survival situation.

"Sometimes the ride can be a little rough," he warned as he settled in the pilot's seat.

After a minute of adjusting instruments, radio, and wing flaps, he ignited the engine. At first, the engine whine sounded more electric than gasoline-powered. The prop, visible through the cockpit window, barely seemed to move, but after a few moments, it was whirring so fast as to be a blur. I lifted my ear protection to hear how loud was the sound it made. I only lifted it an inch before having to pop it back on. The noise was stupendous. The headsets did an excellent job.

Wearing headsets for hearing protection from the roar of the aircraft engine.

We listened in to Michael's communication with the control tower. He allowed us to hear it but our microphones were disconnected so we couldn't disrupt tower and aircraft communication. Pilot and tower traded a few technical terms, and then Michael announced that we were headed to Denali.

"Six out, one back," he said, referring to himself on the return flight. No one would be flying back with him from Denali.

Michael throttled up the engine and we rumbled down the taxiway. Once we turned left from the hangar area, we rolled parallel to the runway. After checking in all directions, he steered the Otter onto the runway. As the aircraft had a tail wheel, all I could see was sky through the cockpit window, so my best view was out a side window.

The engine came to a full roar. For a moment, we didn't move. Then Michael dropped a lever and the plane jumped forward. The acceleration shoved me into my seat back. The force wasn't that of a slingshot roller coaster, but it was much stronger than a Boeing 737 during takeoff. We zoomed along the concrete and in what seemed to be only ten seconds or so we were airborne and rising rapidly above Talkeetna.

My window filled with blue sky as the plane banked right. We made the single turn and then we were on our way to the Alaska Range. After a few minutes of flying over sparse houses and roads, we began to cross the tundra. Islands of green conifers were interspersed between spidery threads of rivers and streams that laced the landscape.

It seemed an infinite plain of trees, rivers, lakes, and bogs that stretched to an absurdly flat horizon.

The tundra soon gave way to the mountains. At first small streaks of snow appeared in channels of rocky dirt. They looked as though they had been scraped by a massive rake. After another thirty seconds, the land rose up and became completely covered in snow. The first granite mountains appeared. Rising up out of the tundra, they looked as though they were protecting an inner winter fortress. The scene reminded me of something out of Tolkien's *Lord of the Rings*.

The glacier we flew over was massive. It looked to be more than two miles wide. The impression it gave was of a river that had been instantly frozen and covered in eternal snow. Massive crags of mountains, jagged and forbidding, silently slipped by the aircraft. Ridge after ridge passed by as we penetrated deeper into the heart of the range.

As we entered the glacier region, Michael announced his position to other pilots in the area. He repeatedly broadcast our location, bearing, and altitude and checked out the window, glancing this way and that, watching for other aircraft that might be in the area. Although the mountain range was vast, common flight paths dictated that other planes may be nearby, so a pilot had to remain alert at all times. I wondered how many near-misses had happened over the years.

Michael called over the headset to point out Denali as it came into view. All of us tugged at our seat belts to look through the cockpit window for the massif. With all of the instruments and gear in the way, viewing Denali through the cockpit window was like looking through a porthole.

"Michael," I requested over the intercom, "would you mind turning to starboard?"

This would allow me and the other climbers in the main cabin a better view of Denali. He didn't hesitate for a moment.

"K2 Foxtrot six-niner making maneuvers," Michael announced to all aircraft in the area.

The plane swung gently to starboard until we were broadside to Denali. Everyone in the back was glued to their window. The mountain towered over all the others around it. It looked exactly like the photographs I had studied but was much more magnificent in person somehow.

After maneuvering around for a better look, Michael resumed our course toward the base camp on the massive Kahiltna Glacier. We flew over the glacier for some time, moving deeper into the mountain range. Farther in, the glacier was still wider than the Mississippi River and was far more impressive. There were crevasses everywhere, and many areas looked utterly impassible. There were also icefalls at the base of many of the mountains. As we flew past seemingly countless granite spires, I wondered how many of them had been climbed. Had humans been up all of these peaks as they had been in the other forty-eight states?

We made our first turn, circling in toward the still invisible landing strip. Looking outside, my eyes widened. I saw a track left by climbers crossing the glacier, leading toward camp 1 at 7,800 feet. Excitement welled up inside me. I had the chance to inspect the route from the air before actually being on it.

Taking several photographs, I made mental notes about several crevasse hazards as we flew along the track. Some were obvious. Others were only visible from the air, as slight indentations in the snow. They would look like inconsequential undulations in the ice at ground level, but at 1,000 feet above the surface, the telltale pattern of crevasses was easily discerned.

Climbing trail across the Kahiltna glacier.

As we turned toward the runway, the glacier loomed large before the aircraft. The closer we came to the runway, the more it filled the cockpit window. It was as though we were diving straight for it, more steeply than I'd ever experienced before in an aircraft. I knew the landing was uphill into the glacier, but it looked much steeper than I'd anticipated.

As the plane's skis hit the ice, Michael throttled back the engine. The thump and grind sounded like we'd landed on a gravel road. The landing felt at least as rough as when I landed at Hercules Inlet in Antarctica. The single-engine Otter rumbled, thudded, and rocked back and forth as we glided over the ice, slowing down with each passing second.

There was no roar from the engine as Michael reduced the propeller angle to reduce our speed but the slope of the glacier did most of the work to slow us down. Kahiltna Glacier base camp came into view through the window as we turned to the left. Michael swung the plane around to face down the glacier and brought us to a gentle stop, then cut power to the engine. Everyone simultaneously unbuckled their seat belts.

"Welcome to Kahiltna Glacier!" Michael chimed over the headsets. "As soon as I get the door open and the ladder in place, please form a line so we can unload the plane."

Michael came down the center aisle and cracked open the door. I expected a huge rush of cold air to fill the cabin, as I had experienced in Antarctica. Instead, nothing happened. The weather was calm outside and the air was warm. He hooked the red ladder to the side of the plane and beckoned at us to deplane.

I shuffled to the door in my unwieldy climbing boots. Conscious of their awkwardness, I gingerly lowered myself out of the aircraft. The steps were easy to see and feel, but I didn't want to stumble and fall onto Denali. Then I quickly walked to the back of the line to help unload the gear.

The pilot hoisted each backpack, fuel box, and sled out to the waiting line of climbers. Initially, we all worked together, bucket-brigading the climbing gear out of the plane. Then, two of the climbers grabbed their backpacks and walked off, content they had everything, leaving the rest of us to finish unloading. It wasn't worth getting upset about. The pair chatted cheerily in their own language as they walked away.

"I guess it's every man for himself out here," one of the others said, to no one in particular.

"Apparently it is," I agreed.

In a few minutes, we had finished unloading. I stood dumbstruck at the scale of the rock faces towering over us. Everything surrounding us was so dramatic.

"Hello, everyone, welcome to Kahiltna Glacier and Denali!" a young woman said as she approached our group. "Does everyone have their fuel cards so we can get you provisioned for your trek?"

I nodded along with everyone else.

"Great! Let me explain to you which tents are ours and how this all works."

Lisa went into detail about which tent belonged to K2 Aviation, and what the contact hours were when we returned from our climb. She also discussed the camp areas, where not to be on the runway, and how the camp operated.

"Unless it's an emergency, please don't come up well after hours to schedule your outbound flight," she said, smiling. "You might find yourself on the bottom of the list."

A laugh rippled through the group. She led us to the supply tent and handed us our fuel can after inspecting our fuel cards.

"Let me know if you have any other questions," Lisa said.

Her words were cut off by the sound of a roaring crash and a rumbling. The sound rippled up the glacier from Mt. Foraker. Everyone stopped to look at the mountain face, trying to discern where the avalanche was. It roared on for nearly a minute before quietening down.

"How often does that happen?" I asked.

"All day, every day," Lisa replied.

"Whoa," was all I could muster.

She excused herself and disappeared into a red hut tent to take care of the flight operations.

I walked the steel gallon can of Coleman white gas fuel back to my sled. Here I was, on Kahiltna Glacier, ready to climb Denali.

I had no plan as to what to do next.

"Guess I should've thought this out a bit better," I said to the clear blue sky.

The Denali guidebook suggested teams stay at base camp for a day to acclimate. It also emphasized the importance of practicing crevasse rescue techniques. There was no lack of them to test skills in.

Since I was acclimated to 10,000 feet and I had no one to practice crevasse rescue with, there was no point in staying at base camp. I looked around, admiring the scenery. Insanely steep rock faces boxed in the glacier and nothing about the sheer granite faces suggested easy or safe travel. Even though I'd studied Bradford Washburn's photographs and the Denali climbing book extensively, I was mentally unprepared for how large and how sheer the cliffs looked here. No one else seemed phased by the view, though.

"It's all in your head, Linsdau," I told myself. "Thousands have successfully followed this route. Many solo climbers have come before me. Let's get started."

Unloading the four one-liter bottles and funnel, I carefully transferred the fuel from the steel can to the plastic bottles. I did this for two reasons. One, I didn't want to haul a steel can up the mountain. Any extra weight was a burden. And two, I didn't want to have the steel can split and leak in a tumble. It's happened to other climbers and polar explorers. If the steel cracked and leaked fuel, I would be in serious trouble as I would have no way to make water. The white gas would also destroy all of my equipment.

I walked over and knocked on the K2 Aviation tent door. Lisa pried open the flap.

"Where should I put the empty fuel can?"

"What happened to all of your fuel," Lisa said in a panic.

"I transferred it to plastic bottles."

She looked at me for a moment, as though I was speaking an alien language.

"I'm solo. If I break that can, I'm toast."

"That makes sense," she said as she pondered the idea.

"Polar exploration taught me to plan for the worst."

"Please put it over there," she said, gesturing to the side of the tent.

"Thank you. Have a great evening!"

"You, too. Good luck."

I did as she instructed and then stuffed the fuel bottles into the back of the sled. Everything was in place. I thought about staying the night at base camp and then decided against it. The weather was perfect, the air was cool, and the sun skimmed the peaks thousands of feet overhead. Even though it was 6:00 p.m., I wanted to take advantage of the weather. There was no reason for me to stay at camp.

It was thrilling to be on this mountain after having first seen it over a decade ago. I realized I was about to set out on my first major solo mountaineering expedition. I was about to climb Denali! I wasn't sure what to expect, other than tough travel, poor weather, and a spectacular challenge. The air was still. A half-dozen people milled around base camp. I would have to snowshoe five miles to reach camp 1, half of it downhill and the other half going moderately upward.

It was time to begin my expedition.

Climbers departing base camp on Denali at 7,200 feet.

Clipping my orange 6mm accessory cord to the locking Black Diamond carabiner and screwing it shut, I linked my backpack to the sled. The sled traces had figure of eight knots and a bungee line woven into it to cut the impact on my back as I walked.

Should I fall through a snow bridge into a crevasse, there were several scenarios that might play out. The first would be that only my legs would punch through the snow. My feet would dangle above death, but I'd be able to drag myself back out.

A less desirable scenario was that I would fall through so that I'd be left sitting in my harness, but saved by the knots cutting into the snow. The sled was heavy enough that it should dig in. My plan then would be to push and swing until I could punch my ice axe into the crevasse wall and hold myself to it. I would then screw in my ice screws and climb my way out.

The worst-case scenario would be to fall through a snow bridge over a large crevasse, in which case my sled might fall with me. In the book *Minus 148°* by Art Davidson, one of the climbers died from a fall into a fifty-foot deep crevasse. Another one fell in but was rescued by his climbing partners. Assuming that I didn't die in the initial fall, my seventy-pound sled would land on me to finish the job. If, somehow, I survived both the fall and the sled impact, I planned to use ice screws to climb my way out of the crevasse. As I didn't have a long climbing rope with me, I would have little chance of dragging my sled back to the surface.

Countless teams have self-rescued their own. As a solo climber, my plan was to follow the established trail and avoid falling through in the first place. I knew falls were a possibility, but I would follow where everyone else had walked to reduce my chance of falling through.

Though it's possible to fall through a snow bridge that everyone else has walked over, it's not very likely. I planned to travel on snowshoes at all times. Once I reached the upper mountain, I would switch to crampons. Walking alone without skis or snowshoes on a glacier is an invitation to be killed. I had no desire to disappear into a blue-black void.

Crevasses on the Kahiltna glacier viewed from a thousand feet above.

The nice part about leaving base camp was the downhill trek. Once I reached 7,000 feet, every step I took would be uphill. The steepest slope on this route was 50°. I looked forward to it after the months of training.

Following everyone else's tracks, I headed down Heartbreak Hill. In minutes, I was alone, the only person on the trail. The scale of the mountains surrounding me was surreal. They almost looked fake. Much of the glacier was encased by sheer cliffs thousands of feet high.

Black granite towered above me, with seracs of blue ice and snow dangling precariously from every rock face. There was no sense of scale. Although the blocks of ice looked small, when I spotted climbers near them they looked like ants. Those little chunks of ice were, in fact, the size of skyscrapers.

My mind became absorbed in "what-if" disaster scenarios once again.

The "what-if" that particularly occupied my mind was "What if that block gave way? Was I far enough away to survive?" I had no way of knowing. As I continued my way down, I heard the crash of another avalanche rumbling across the Kahiltna Glacier, somewhere out of sight. Once the last sounds had died away, I stopped for a moment to bask in the silence. It was similar to Antarctica. No matter how much I yelled, I heard nothing. No sound bounced back to me. It was as though I was in space. I realized that, should I be in trouble and yell for help, no one would hear me.

In the distance, I saw a single tent at the lowest point on the trail. It looked tiny, and it took forty-five minutes of continuous snowshoeing to reach it. The German couple I found there warned me of the dangers at hand.

"Please be careful," said the man in German-accented English. "My wife broke through a snow bridge."

"Oh no, was she hurt at all? Do you need help?"

"No, not at all. Thank you. That was two hours ago. We marked the spots with wands. She was uninjured and we're fine now. Are you alone?"

"Yes, I'm out here solo."

"Wow. Be careful, there are many crevasses—as we discovered."

"Good to know. Thank you for the warning. Have a good night."

"You, too. Good luck."

I waved goodbye and marched on toward camp 1 at 7,900 feet. After fifteen minutes of walking, I looked back. The German camp had disappeared into a light fog and the sun had fallen behind the surrounding cliffs. In minutes the temperature plummeted fifteen degrees, cooling me off. Although I was walking downhill, dragging the sled took effort. I had stripped down to my shell pants and ExOfficio button-down shirt at the German camp. Now I reversed the process, adding my REI eVent shell to ward off the chill. A slight breeze numbed my fingers, forcing me to put on gloves. The shift from being too warm to cool was fast. It surprised me how quickly temperatures changed hereabouts.

I smiled as I walked along the footpath toward Camp 1. Here I was, alone in the Alaska Range, tramping on the West Buttress Route toward my first attempt on Denali's summit. Fog and cloud obscured the upper glacier so there was no way to see what I was in for. I was glad for this for I didn't want to see how much mountain I had to climb. I didn't want to battle discouragement too early. Looking at something too big is overwhelming. It was much easier to focus on the task at hand.

Other than the crunch of my snowshoes and the "ziff-ziff" sounds of my nylon clothing, there was no sound at all. Neither were there any smells. Only the dry, icy coolness of the glacial air filled my nostrils. Now the sun had disappeared behind the mountains, I removed my sunglasses. The sky was still bright, but the glasses made it too dark to see what I was doing and they made the surrounding mountains look gray and muddy. Although the cool air-dried my eyes, I dealt with the discomfort. I wanted to see everything.

After an additional two hours of snowshoeing, I arrived at Camp 1. It had only taken five hours to travel five miles on the glacier, half downhill and the other half uphill. Before pitching my tent, I probed diligently around my campsite with my trekking poles. I didn't want to end up sleeping on an unseen crevasse and fall into it at 3:00 a.m. Like a mummy, I would be trapped inside my sleeping bag, wrapped inside my tent, and entombed in ice. It was the perfect nightmare scenario for a claustrophobic.

Although I was tired, I had to boil water for dinner. It was late and I didn't feel like it, but I knew that without warm food, I would be cold during the night and would wake up nauseatingly hungry. I pulled one of my ration bags out at random and, after melting and boiling some snow for half an hour, tucked into some freeze-dried spaghetti.

There was no wind, so I enjoyed the view through the unzipped door of the tent, though most of what I saw was a wall of rock and ice. Everything stretched so high here. The only way to see the top of anything was to poke my head out of the tent and look nearly straight up.

After brushing my teeth and changed out of my clothing, I bedded down in my jade green Western Mountaineering -25° Puma down sleeping bag. Here I was, making my first solo climb of Denali. I was having the time of my life.

I whispered, "Welcome to Alaska," as I fell asleep.

Camp 1, 7,800 feet. The tent was half pitched when I took the picture before it became too dark.

～

Dropping into the unknown is often overwhelming. Obstacles will initially appear insurmountable. Don't lose heart, as the road is long.

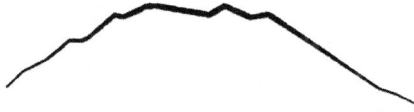

CHAPTER 5

May 11
7.9k camp to 9k camp
Whiteout

When I woke, I undid the draw cord on the sleeping bag in an attempt to see what the world had in store for me today. Wriggling around to get myself out of my cocoon of feathers, I dislodged a pancake of frost from the tent wall. It fell from the ceiling and plopped on my face.

"Welcome to Denali," my tent said.

The icy facemask had me fully awake in an instant. I shoved a hand out of the small opening in the sleeping bag and rubbed the ice off my face. My red tent rippled in the morning breeze and I could see there were several other patches of ice dangling from the fabric above me, waiting for the opportunity to liven up my morning even more.

Even though the air was dry, my exhalations and the warmth of my body had been enough to heat up the water vapor and fuse it to the tent. Overnight, those droplets of water had combined to form a coating similar to paint. By the time I woke up at 6:00 a.m., the ice was as thick as a tortilla. For some reason, I find the wind never seems to dislodge these accumulations of ice. Only when I do something to disturb them do they drop off, invariably onto my face.

Fog had descended during the night and I saw that I was in a complete whiteout now morning had come. When I stuck my head out the door, all I could see was a grayish haze. It was so thick I couldn't even see the blue of the sky filtering through. Looking up and downhill, the trail was nearly invisible in both directions. I knew there were wands marking the trail, and I hoped that whoever had been courteous enough to mark the trail had continued their efforts all the way up the mountain. I didn't want to be lost on a crevassed glacier inside a cloud.

The temperature was only 0°F and the icy chill made me want to remain in my sleeping bag until the sun rose properly. My sleeping bag was comfort-rated to –20°F. The difference left me with plenty of latitude for warmth. If this was the coldest Denali became, I'd made the right decision in not bringing my –40° expedition bag.

I wanted to get started in the coolness of dawn, however, so I decided against waiting for the sun to rise over the invisible cliffs above me. My first priority was to scrape off all the ice coating the tent's insides. If I didn't, it would fill the inside of my sleeping bag with frost. That in turn would melt from the remaining warmth of the bag, soaking the precious down.

The outside of the sleeping bag was waterproof but the inside liner was not. Although down is the warmest known insulator, moisture is its weakness. Should down become wet, it retains no heat. On the other hand, wool retains its warmth whether it's dry or wet. One might argue that a wool sleeping bag would be better than down, but therein lies the rub. Down is the best insulator for its weight. The biggest consideration is how much insulation a material provides compared to how much it weighs. Pound for pound, airy tufts of goose down are unmatched by any natural or synthetic material. For the millions of dollars spent on synthetic insulation research, nothing has matched the weight versus warmth performance of down.

Opening a ration bag, I dug through and found my cereal pouch. In the Press-and-Seal makeshift bag was a full serving of granola, three teaspoons of sugar, and enough whole powdered milk to make eight ounces of milk. The whole mess provided 500 calories, enough to fuel me into the late morning. I carefully poured the messy dust into my dark gray Lexan mug, topping it up with water. Using my titanium spoon, I wolfed down the crunchy mix, calming my growling stomach.

Why didn't I heat up water in the morning to make a hot breakfast? Over years of trekking in winter conditions, I've found the comfort of a hot breakfast isn't worth the extra time and fuel. Making water the night before ensures that all I have to do in the morning is to wake up, eat, toilet, and break camp. There is nothing additional to do. My approach is to focus on completing all necessary maintenance tasks at night so my morning is focused.

Every time I fire up the stove, I have to cool it and clean the shaker jet. The pinhole that fuel comes through on a white gas expedition stove builds up carbon deposits. These cause the stove to burn improperly, creating carbon monoxide, a toxic, odorless gas. In the confined space of a tent, it doesn't take long to be poisoned by this gas and to suffocate. Many campers have died from carbon monoxide poisoning. The danger is magnified in the winter, as campers and climbers tend to remain inside their tents and cook inside them as well. As a general rule this is a no-no, but when the air is subzero and there are gale force winds, cooking outside can become all but impossible.

After completing my morning activities, I stepped outside. It looked like the entire mountain range was fogged in and that it would be easy to lose my bearings. I packed up all of my gear for a single haul up to 9.6k camp. Often times teams use a technique called double-hauling. This is where they drag or carry some supplies up to the next campsite, then descend again to sleep. The axiom for high altitude mountaineering is to climb high and sleep low. This process gives the body time to adjust to the increasingly thin air as a climber ascends, a process called acclimation.

Should a climber ascend too quickly, acute mountain sickness (AMS), high altitude pulmonary or cerebral (HAPE, HACE), may develop. AMS is an annoyance and common on high climbs. It makes one feel hung over, with headaches, lethargy, loss of appetite, and nausea. The symptoms usually subside in a few days.

HACE and HAPE are entirely different and lethal matters. HACE is caused by the brain swelling from the lack of oxygen. In severe cases, fluid builds up in the brain, causing disorientation, inability to think, and ultimately death. Though uncommon below 13,000 feet, it does happen. The initial symptoms are similar to AMS. The difference is, a climber with AMS feels bad whereas one with HACE rapidly loses mental acuity. Should symptoms become severe, a disoriented climber will have extreme difficulty walking down a mountain under their own power. There is no way to determine who is susceptible to this condition. Once the condition develops, the climber must descend quickly. Otherwise, death is common within forty-eight hours.

HAPE is caused by the same lack of oxygen as HACE. In this instance, the body's negative reaction to oxygen starvation causes a build-up of fluid in the lungs. This dangerous condition occurs above 8,000 feet, where climbers spend most of their time on Denali. No one knows what makes some more susceptible than others. Again, the only treatment is to descend rapidly. As with HACE, if a climber suffers from severe HAPE, solo descent may be difficult if not impossible.

All of these dangers were on my mind as a solo climber on Denali. My solution to these dangers was to acclimate in Jackson by climbing Mt. Glory to 10,000 feet during training. I climbed this mountain four times per week before coming to Alaska. Though acclimation only lasts one to two weeks, my experience of climbing Orizaba (18,491 feet) taught me that this pre-acclimation technique was effective. I had planned to single-haul all the way to the camp at 11,000 feet before resorting to double-hauling the rest of the mountain.

Climbers often joke that Denali has to be climbed twice. One day is spent climbing up, caching supplies, and then descending. The next day is spent returning to the previous day's altitude. For most climbers, this approach is effective and safe. The thought of repeatedly climbing back and forth, however, was demoralizing.

After a few hundred feet of travel, I began climbing Ski Hill. The fog was thick and the blowing snow made for poor visibility. Every time I reached a wand, I had to stand for a minute or longer until I spotted the next marker. The previous climbers' tracks were fully obscured by the whiteout and I did not want to climb off route and fall into an unmarked crevasse. No one would follow my wayward tracks to find out what happened to me. Only after I didn't return at my appointed time (June 1) would the park service initiate a search. Should I survive the initial fall, my tracks would be long gone and with them any clue as to my whereabouts. As a solo climber, staying on the route was paramount to safety and possible rescue.

Looking for thin bamboo wands in a white haze was trying. Finding them on a steep hill was additionally complex, as I wasn't exactly sure where to look. There was nothing to look at but gray. My eyes defocused. Even when I stared directly at a wand, I couldn't see it. I had to consciously drive the focus of my eyes from near to far in order to spot the next wand.

Though the effort burned no calories, it wore me down. Up to this point, the black shafts of bamboo had been spaced between fifty to one hundred yards. Finding them would have been easier on flat ground because I would only need to look in one direction. But Ski Hill was steep, so I had to look both back and forth as well as up and down. Blind climbing made the experience much more intense.

After climbing the first section of the hill, I found a relatively flat spot and rested. With the wind swirling snow around me, it would be easy to become lost. Though I knew I would be traveling up another hill, determining the exact direction was difficult. It only took an error of a few degrees to end up off course. I took a bearing with my compass to guard against just such an occurrence. The plastic base chilled to 0°F in the few moments it was in the wind. When I put it back in my shirt, it seared my chest.

"Ooh! Aah!" I yelled as I danced around. "That was freezing!"

While climbing the second hill in what felt like a gathering storm, a dark shape the size of a book flew by my head twice. With blowing snow and my goggles on, whatever it was scared me. I flinched by jerking my head back as it flew by the second time. Was something trying to land on my head? Then, after a few disorienting moments, an American robin startled me by landing next to my sled. Should the little bird not have chirped, I wouldn't have believed it was real. Hopping this way and that, it seemed to be trying to find shelter from the wind behind my sled.

"How in the world did a robin end up in the middle of the Alaska Range?" I asked myself. Perhaps it had been blown in by the storm?

I felt bad for the poor little beast. It was miles from the nearest trees or grass. There was nothing for it here to survive on. I thought about tossing it some seeds from a granola bar, even though I knew that robins eat bugs, worms, and berries.

After a minute of whistling and hopping back and forth, it flew off. Vaulting back into the air, it spun twice and zoomed past my head. I pulled on my goggles and strained to see where it went. But, looking all around the solid blanket of white, I saw nothing. The wind made it equally impossible to hear its voice or the beat of its wings. It was gone, as though it had never existed. I questioned my sanity for a moment. Had seeing ravens in the middle of Antarctica permanently affected my mind?

Climbing up the second hill was easier than the first, as thoughts of the robin kept me company. It never returned but I thought I saw it while looking for wands. Eventually, the trail markers led me to the plateau. At that exact moment, the clouds rose off the ground.

"Woo hoo!" I yelled out.

I saw the trail followed a rolling hill, rising slowly up the glacier. Though the sun was hidden, I could see the trail, so sunlight must be penetrating the trail ahead. As I continued my way up, the wind-blown tracks flitted in and out of view. It was as though someone placed and removed a sheet of paper in front of my face. Grinning, I enjoyed the peculiar effect on my mind.

At 3:00 p.m., I found an encampment, but it was abandoned. With no climbers in sight, I had the chance to inspect each snow wall and chose the best. There were caves, pits, half igloos, and several walls to choose from. Although I would have preferred to sleep in one of the pits, each was soiled by human waste. I didn't want to sleep exposed to the wind, but there was no complete igloo or snow pit providing complete protection. Should the wind shift at night, I would have an unpleasant night.

After choosing a snow wall, I thoroughly stabbed the surrounding snow with my trekking poles to check for any undetected crevasse. I was glad to find nothing. As exciting as I would be to punch through a crevasse, I wouldn't be able to sleep knowing I was near one. My mind would be filled with thoughts of falling into an abyss.

Once I had camp set and was eating dinner, the first set of climbers I'd seen all day passed by. I waved when they stopped and a few waved back. They all spoke German. It was difficult to hear them, however, over the flapping of my tent.

Not interested in setting camp, they moved on. I expected many more climbers to pass by. Just like last night, there were few climbers on the lower section of the mountain. I enjoyed the solitude, as I was sure to be surrounded by others higher up. Denali regularly sees a thousand climbers per season. Most come in late May and early June.

Throughout the night, the wind whipped at my tent, making a racket. I stuffed silicone earplugs in to ward off the noise. I also wore my eye mask in case the sky cleared, as being woken up by blinding light makes sleep difficult. I wanted a solid night's rest in order to be refreshed for the climb tomorrow.

~

After starting in sunshine and light winds, the reality of what you're undertaking will catch up with you. You will feel like you're wandering blind surrounded by danger. Keep moving forward and correct your course as you go along.

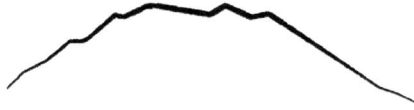

CHAPTER 6

May 12
Side wind to 11k

No other climbers were out wandering camp at 5:00 a.m. In fact, not much at all was visible in the blue-gray morning light. Wriggling out of my tent, I scanned the area. No one had built a camp near me last night. I was happy for the silence but a little disappointed that there was no one to chat with about climbing. I really felt alone, like I was the only climber on the mountain. But the feeling wasn't negative, as in being abandoned. Rather, it was a sense of being by myself on a massive mountain, battling my way up. There was nothing unpleasant about the feeling at all. I was perfectly comfortable with the isolation after having been on so many solo treks.

The distance I had to travel that day was trivial, only three horizontal miles. In fact, the total distance to the peak from base camp was a mere fifteen miles. I could cover that distance horizontally with a fifty-pound pack in a day. It was the vertical elevation gain and absolute altitude that mattered.

The 11k camp was the first camp that *Denali's West Buttress* suggested double carrying to. As I had climbed to 10,000 feet only a week before the climb, I shouldn't have too much trouble at this elevation. I opted to single-haul (haul all gear in a single push to the next camp) to 11k camp. This would make the day longer and tougher, but it would pay off in reducing the number of days I had to travel.

Six hours of climbing sounds like a lot, but it isn't. Every day in Antarctica requires nine hours of skiing. Though summit days can take twenty-four hours, the days are never long on Denali. Though this mountain has a reputation for being one of the toughest, the shorter days make it feel easier. That said, the work of climbing is still grueling. Distance and time don't matter here—only elevation gain does. The constant steep slopes make all the difference.

When I departed at 9:00 a.m., the sun had not yet risen over the ridge above me. When it finally did, it failed to penetrate the soupy clouds blanketing the lower glacier. The effect was surreal. When the sun did show through, the trail materialized and was easy to follow. Every few minutes, however, the clouds thickened, choking off the sun, and the tracks vanished. I stopped to stare intently at the horizon, sleuthing for marker wands. Once my eyes focused on one, I marched another seventy yards. The cycle repeated for hours. Meanwhile, the wind increased.

"At least it's a tailwind," I said to the sky. The inconsistent wind made Denali feel out of control, but coping with them made the climbing experience more interesting and enjoyable. I never knew what I was going to encounter compared to my experience in Antarctica. The Alaska Range was a different animal, not at all like the polar regions. My three months of polar living had created a flawed vision of weather consistency in my mind. I delved now into the mindset of Denali, where anything can come from anywhere.

After hours of towing my sled into the fog, a large group of climbers appeared in the distance. At first, they were a formless, gray mass on an otherwise blank canvas. As I drew near, they became more distinct. Only when I was within one hundred feet of them was I able to identify the color of their outerwear. Two of the climbers were in a hole, digging, while the rest stood around. They looked like a street repair crew, the kind you'd find in any city, though not far up in the Alaska Range.

My altimeter indicated I had reached 10,000 feet above sea level. I had finally reached a real milestone after two days of climbing. Stopping twenty feet away to take a food and water break, I sat down to observe the group's machinations. Two of the climbers were clearly guides, doing the hard work while their clients watched. They were exhuming their cache and preparing to drag it higher. I surmised they had hiked up yesterday, dropped a batch of supplies, and continued on up. This reduced their weight on their final 1,000 foot climb to 11k camp.

I debated leaving a small cache of supplies here as well. I expected to descend from the summit in two weeks. If all went well, I would need two days of rations at that point. This was the perfect place to drop them. The area was flat and used by others for the same purpose, so losing my cache seemed unlikely. I wanted to shed a few pounds, so dropping a cache here seemed an obvious thing to do.

Dredging the orange aluminum avalanche shovel out of my red sled bag, I set about digging a hole. It needed to be deep enough to protect my supplies from the ravens. Multiple reports have shown that these persistent birds raid shallow burials. The additional depth is also important to safeguard against melting. Online blogs of other climbers relate how their caches were exposed after being buried only two feet under the snow. However, I didn't want to bury the supplies so deep as to make them irretrievable. I had spent a good while observing what other professionally guided teams had done.

As I dug my unscientifically calculated hole depth, the guided group broke into two separate climbing parties. Each person was tied into one long 11mm climbing rope with their carabiner clipped into an alpine butterfly knot.

Alpine butterfly knot

Each party had a total of five climbers with a guide in the lead. As the wind had risen to storm level, each person faced the ground as the others clipped in and prepared to ascend. The wind was blowing the snow horizontally, but the sun illuminated the trail, making navigation easier. One of the guides started yelling to the rest of the team.

"Make sure you put on your balaclava. Once we turn up the mountain, the wind blows from the right. You'll get windburn or frostbite on your cheek if you're not fully protected."

Only when I heard her voice did I realize the guide was female. Other than her small stature and the slightly feminine color of her down jacket, there was nothing to indicate the guide's gender. Climbing clothing tends to be generic, so a fully dressed woman, especially if tall in stature, can easily be mistaken for a man.

Everyone heeded the guide's warning. They dug into pockets, drew out hoods and other protection, and pulled them on. Looking at them, I could only imagine overheating. Even if I climbed extra slowly, I'd overheat with a neck gaiter, balaclava, hood, and a climbing helmet.

"Let's head out," the other guide, a man, hollered over the gusting wind.

The chain gang of climbers faced uphill and prepared for their battle into the storm. The guide started out first, then, as the rope became nearly taut, the next climber began marching. The rhythm was repeated until all climbers were moving. All kept their faces down. Loaded with large packs, they looked like slaves falling into line. It was impossible to see their expressions, so I couldn't discern if any of them was having a good time or not.

By the time I had finished digging my hole, the climbing teams were nearly out of sight. They soon turned up the hill and disappeared from view. I wanted to follow their tracks so I didn't become lost in the building storm. I hurriedly jammed several bamboo wands into the snow, one with my National Park Service sticker, and rammed everything into my sled bag. Powering up my GPS, I marked a waypoint on the unit. This allowed me to find my supplies should the markers be destroyed or buried.

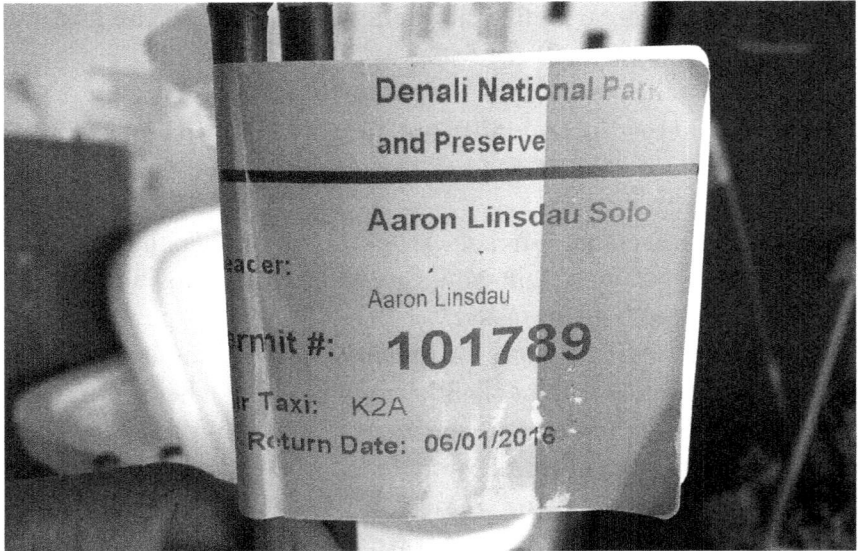

Hoisting my backpack, I began plodding after the guided teams. Looking back at my cache, I wondered when and if I would see it again. I was certain no one would mess with it, but I still wondered how it would fare in the two weeks that I would be away.

As I snowshoed up the slope toward the ridge, I saw three birds fly past, high in the sky. They seemed able to keep their bearings regardless of the wind. Sometimes they were caught by gusts, but they adjusted to them with ease and returned to their aerial route. As I watched them, a strong gust blew snow up into the air around me. The birds vanished from sight. When the air cleared, they were gone.

Had I really seen them or was this another illusion? After hallucinating in Antarctica, I was not confident of my senses. Every time things randomly appeared and disappeared, I questioned my sanity. Smiling, I embraced the visions in my mind—if the birds were a figment, then they were a joyous one to imagine.

As I reached the crest of the ridge, I donned my facemask and goggles, ready to do battle with the elements. Now out of sight of my cache, I made the right turn toward 11k camp. Just as the guide predicted, the wind blew from the right, chilling my nose, cheek, and right eye. I longed for the fur ruff of my polar parka. The hair would have blocked the wind and stopped it reaching my face.

After a few minutes of climbing uphill, my goggles fogged. I was generating too much heat. Pulling back my climbing hood to cool down, snow blew into my jacket.

"No, that's not going to work," I said to myself. The filtered snow in my shell chilled me too much. Pulling the hood back on, I unzipped the front of the jacket. Deciding how much to expose my body to the elements was difficult. Too much and I shivered. Too covered up and I overheated. The wind gusted, making any decision all the more challenging. All the while, my goggles fogged up, obliterating my view.

"I love it. Bring it on!" I yelled. This was what I was climbing Denali for—to find where my edge was, to challenge myself to see if I could deal with whatever was thrown at me.

Unable to clear my goggles, I took them off and switched to glasses. Soon, they too fogged up. I pulled them slightly away from my face in order to prevent them from icing over. They cleared but I was now getting snow in my eyes and ice was forming on my eyelashes. "This is the best time ever," I thought.

At one point I took a break and a lightly loaded climbing team passed me. Smiling, I said hello to everyone who passed.

"Are you alone?" several asked with incredulity.

"Yes, and it's a wonderful day to be climbing Denali solo," I jested.

"Have fun," replied one of them.

"Sure will," was all I could get out before they were dragged along by the rest of the team.

A few other climbers ignored me, instead focusing gamely on their every step. I hoped they were having a good time despite the roaring storm.

It took a solid hour of climbing to reach the left turn to head into 11k camp. I saw the team ahead of me make the turn, so I had a good idea where it was. Coombs's *Denali West Buttress* described this area as being full of "ghost wands." That is, people who had become lost in poor visibility had poked wands into the snow wherever they thought necessary. Fortunately the line of wands ahead of me looked consistent and easy to follow. Perhaps more teams plant wands as they climb through the turn later in the season.

I enjoyed brief moments of respite whenever the wind fell. They never lasted long, however, before they were followed by roaring gales that forced me to stop and look away. The variation in the wind blasting over the ridge was amazing. My right side was fairly covered in ice, hardening my jacket into a stiff nylon sheet. As soon as I made the left turn, with the wind now at my back, the ice broke off, freeing me from the weight. Instead, my backpack took the brunt of the storm's onslaught.

In fifteen minutes, I reached the outskirts of 11k camp and stopped. The effort of towing a seventy pound sled and carrying a fifty pound pack had taken its toll. All of my joints and muscles ached. Resting for some time, I surveyed what I could see of the camp. With wind peeling snow high into the air, much of the camp was indiscernible. Although I was cold from the wind, I didn't move until I understood the layout of the whole area. And it was easy to see how dangerous this camp was.

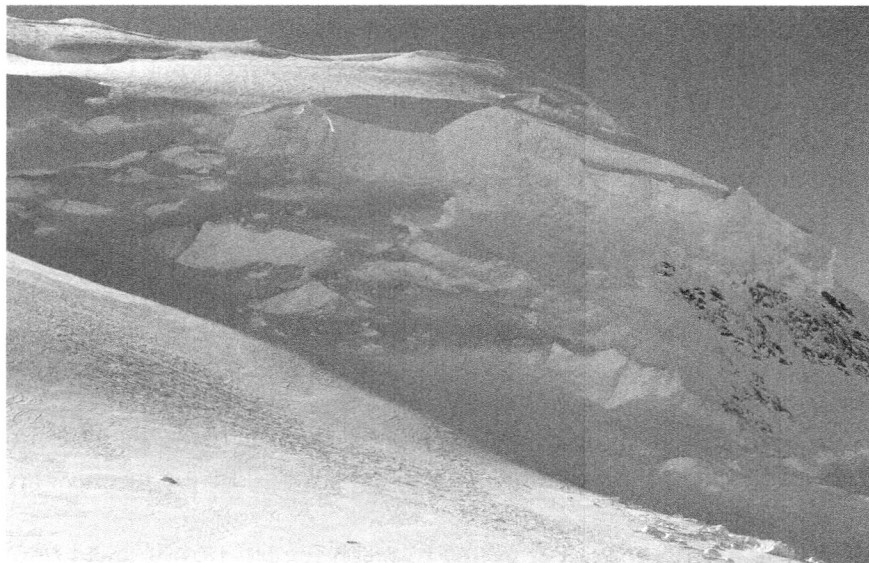

On one side was a wall covered in ice blocks that looked like they could fall at any minute. In the middle of the glacier was a series of crevasses. As a result no one camped in the middle or to the right side of the glacier, meaning there was only a small area that was safe for camping. Coombs's book warned that avalanches can run from the hill above 11k camp all the way down to where my cache was buried. I shuddered at the thought. Should that massive slope break away, everyone here would be swept away and would perish. Part of me liked the risk, but my more emotional side was scared. None of the other climbers appeared concerned. I got moving again and finished my walk toward Motorcycle Hill, blown forward and uphill by the wind.

Passing several tents, I debated where to place mine. I didn't want to be too far down the slope, with more hills to climb in the morning. Nor did I want to be too near the crevasses, as some have opened up right next to tents in previous years. The human waste disposal crevasse was in the center of camp. Its dark maw looked threatening and insidious.

After debating for some time, I settled on camping close to Motorcycle Hill, reducing the amount of slope I would have to climb every time I went anywhere. It also allowed me the chance to talk to everyone who passed and collect information. There was not enough room in the glacier to spread out the camp much. By necessity, most of us were nearly on top of each other.

People relieved themselves in designated sunken-in areas. This kept urine from being spread all over camp. Modesty was not an option as everyone was out where anyone could see their business. Since everyone had to go through the same experience, people actively ignored anyone in a pit. This was all vastly different to my other winter expeditions when I was nearly always by myself with no one for countless miles around.

I attempted to use the abandoned snow wall I had chosen as part of my camp. The tent required a flat area of twelve feet by six feet. The wall itself was tiny. I began digging a pit for the tent. Every other team had dug a pit for their tent, so I thought I should, too. I didn't want to feel the odd man out.

After an hour of digging, I had only half the hole I needed. There were spots of soft snow, but most was rock hard, making shoveling impossible. I used my snow saw to cut a few blocks but found the work laborious and backbreaking, so I stopped.

"What am I doing?" I asked myself. "I survived three months without digging a single pit in Antarctica. And the weather was worse there."

Standing and looking at the half-dug pit, I shook my head. Digging a huge hole in the ice was disheartening and I feared breaking my shovel. Every time I struck ice, the aluminum rang in my hands like a cathedral bell. The snow saw cut the ice at a glacial pace. When I tried chiseling with my steel military folding saw it barely penetrated the ice. I guessed it would take another hour to break enough ice to level out the hole.

This was a job for a team or for someone with an inadequate tent. My Hilleberg Namatjj 2 was "invincible", so why not put my trust in it and use it to my advantage?

Disgusted, I clambered out of the pit. Raising and lowering my shoulders with a sigh, I strapped on the snowshoes. In ten minutes, I had stomped out a flat area. In another ten minutes, I had pitched my tent. Why had I tried to dig a snow pit like everyone else? I knew that I could build a wall from random blocks easier than digging a pit by myself.

Thinking about it for a moment, I saw my error. I was trying to be like everyone else, to do what they did as part of a team. A solo climber has to approach big mountain camping differently. I had to conserve energy. Some will argue it's foolish not to dig a pit. But had I initially stomped out a flat spot and built a blockade instead I would already have been eating and resting. Instead, I had worked for nearly two hours and accomplished little. Relying on my skills and doing what worked for me was a better option. I promised myself not to make the same error for the rest of the climb.

While shoveling snow, I felt incredibly good. Though I was weary, my head and body felt fine. The height I was at didn't bother me. Knowing the altitude might bring on a hangover, however, I swallowed some aspirin. It took a moment to raise the Nalgene to my mouth, so I tasted the full bitterness of the melting pills. The heavy work of single-hauling up the hill would, no doubt, catch up with me tomorrow.

The tent shook violently from the wind while I prepared and ate dinner. I didn't care for, as bad as it felt outside, the conditions weren't really that tough. The gusting nature of the wind made it sound worse than it really was. It was a euphemism for life. Things sound much worse than they really are.

After resting, I climbed back out and shoveled my excavated blocks into a wall. In a few minutes, I had a solid barrier and the flapping of my tent calmed down. This was much easier than digging a pit of despair. I got out my eye mask and earplugs, so no matter how bad the storm might become, I could sleep without disturbance.

I looked up at Squirrel Point, the tell-tale of what Windy Corner was like. Waves of snow were ripping off of it, some hundreds of yards long. I couldn't believe the ferocity of the wind a thousand feet above 11k camp. Coombs's book noted that whatever was visible above 11k camp would continue all the way to 14k camp. Heeding the conditions above Motorcycle Hill was paramount to surviving the next section of the climb. The roar from the winds above was incredible. Wind ripping over the rocks made a stupendous noise, as though there was a waterfall cascading down just outside the camp.

"I wonder what being caught up there in these conditions is like," I murmured to myself.

The strengthening gale carried away my laughter. I might be stuck here for a day or two until conditions improved. As the gusts rose, I fanned my hands out and arced my arms like a windmill. I was having a superb time. The weather was exciting, the climb was difficult, and I had made it this far. I had enough supplies to last for another two weeks on the mountain.

Satisfied with my camp's set-up, I crawled into the tent and bedded down. The sky never went black, so I flopped onto my sleeping bag and stared at the red nylon above me. This was my home and my refuge. No matter how bad the conditions were outside, I was safe inside the Hilleberg. The worst-case scenario was a huge dump of snow. If that happened, all I would need to do was hop out and dig out the tent. I had been warned that a foot or more could fall in the evening. I reveled at the thought. It would make a good story even better.

~

After you have been in the roar of the storm, you have to decide what your attitude will be about it. Both negative and positive feeling will wash over you. Neither is wrong. It's your choice about which you focus on that determines your course.

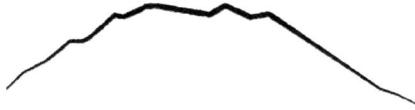

Chapter 7

May 13
First day above 10,000 feet

The next day would be my first above 10,000 feet. I was now living at real altitude. And I felt it. Even when I arrived the previous evening, I knew that it would catch up with me. Single-hauling up the mountain had pushed my body to the limit. Climbing to camp with an eighty pound sled and a fifty pound pack guaranteed that I would be worn out. But in my mind, I had felt it was better to advance as long as I was able, even if it was tough. I would rather be higher on the mountain when poor weather moved in.

My nose was stuffy all night, making sleep nearly impossible. Had I slept better, I might have felt better than I did. But that was a pile of "what-ifs." I was dealing with "what-dids" and "what-are-you-going-to-do-about-its?" It had been a long time since I had camped on a glacier with congestion. Even though I had a cold and bronchitis in Antarctica, it was easy to sleep with a runny nose.

This was different. The symptoms were like I had caught a cold, though I didn't think I had. I was forced to breathe through my mouth the whole night, which meant I became badly dehydrated. I chugged water at regular intervals, but that caused its own problems. I had to relieve myself several times during the night, further cutting into my sleep. My body had gone haywire. I had never thought of bringing a nasal decongestant on a trip like this. I had cold meds to help with a runny nose, but those wouldn't help here.

I didn't want to waste a half roll of toilet paper trying to clear my nose. Those little squares of industrial paper were a critical resource—run out of them and, well, things would be much rougher on the mountain. Instead, I used the polar nose-clearing technique. That is, I grabbed a handful of icy snow, balled it up, jammed it into my face, and blew. Then I hucked the disgusting clump as far away from camp as I could. I repeated the process until I could breathe again. And this repeated planting of my face in the snow worked.

Though the process sounds unpleasant, it relieved the discomfort. The supply of icy snow was infinite, so I never had to worry about running out. Plus, there was the distinct advantage of not chaffing my nose with rough toilet paper. I had suffered on previous winter trips with bleeding and raw nostrils. Once I figured this out, many treks ago, I permanently eliminated a significant source of stress. Minor annoyances at home can turn into major infections in the wild, but I never wasted my valuable toilet paper on my nose. Being careful with resources and my health made the difference between an enjoyable expedition and a painful escapade.

Swallowing two aspirin to reduce the effects of altitude, I wondered what I would do with myself today. I hadn't had a rest day on an expedition not forced by weather or health in years. They were necessary for success on Denali, but it felt strange. It was as though I was wasting time not climbing.

The great danger on high-altitude mountains is climbing too quickly. Coombs's *West Buttress* book warned that climbers have developed serious high-altitude sickness at 11k camp. I took the warning seriously. Though I'd been training to 10,000 feet in Jackson, prematurely advancing higher could result in altitude sickness. Patience was a climber's best friend on this mountain.

After eating breakfast and consuming two liters of water, I felt marginally better.

"Did I make a mistake by moving from 9k to 11k camp in a single haul?" I asked myself. Many other teams climbed up and down to reduce the workload. The idea of going back and forth was utterly unappealing. My only desire was to move forward and do so quickly. This was the first moment of doubt I had had about what I was doing here.

Knowing how dangerous doubt was, I immediately set out to eliminate the feeling. I donned my outer gear and jumped out of the tent. Knowing that action and motion helps humans to acclimate to the altitude, I set out to walk back and forth toward Motorcycle Hill. I took twenty fast steps and nearly passed out. I saw sparkling stars. Leaning over with my hands on my knees, I remembered where I was—near the Arctic Circle.

One of the reasons Denali is difficult to climb is because the atmosphere is thinner near the polar regions. At an equivalent altitude in the lower forty-eight states, there is more oxygen. This mountain is closer to the pole and the altitude I was at felt more like 12,000 feet.

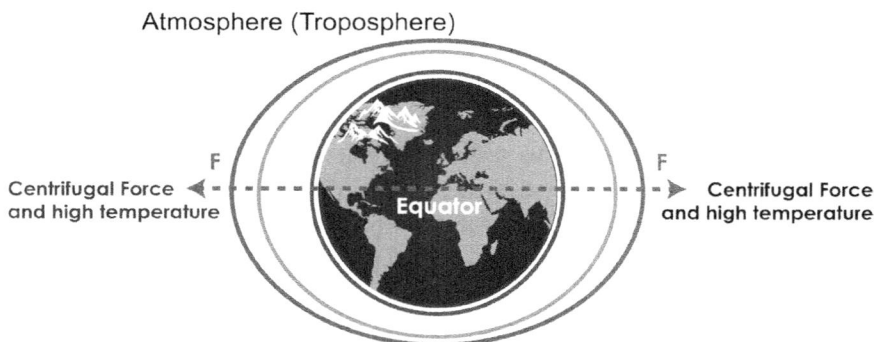

Thinner atmosphere at the poles.

Chastising myself for not walking more slowly, I rested a minute.

"That was dumb," I scolded myself. "Come on, practice your high-altitude techniques."

When I climbed in Mexico with a team lead by Randall Peeters, an Adventure Grand Slam climber, the team forced me to walk slowly. Now, I had to self-regulate my speed. Fully standing up, I practiced pressure breathing to recover my senses. It's a similar action to blowing out a candle. In a few moments, the lightheadedness dissipated.

After letting the annoyance stew for a moment, I washed it off with laughter. I knew to acknowledge my emotions, let them run their course, then cut them off. They are a natural human experience after all. The trick is not to let them run away with you. Visualizing a shower of laughter to scrub off the grime of irritation, a smile returned to my face. The technique is easy to write about but it's another matter to put it into practice. It takes time and patience to master. Sometimes negative emotions still overwhelm me. Staying upset is difficult, though, if you are wearing a smile.

Walking two hundred yards back and forth from camp to the base of Motorcycle Hill made me feel better. My headache subsided and a natural smile returned. I told myself, "Here I am on Denali, climbing solo. Have a good time with it."

Thrusting my hands into the air in triumph, I repeated the mantra, "You will succeed. You are a careful and strong climber. You will make it and return home safely." This positive reinforcement seems goofy but it works. It plants a vision of safety and success in my mind. When climbing alone on a mountain, I need all the positive vision I can muster.

While climbing back and forth, I watched the snow stream off Squirrel Point. Long tails of snow flew off the cliff, hundreds of yards long. That meant climbing up higher was dangerous. If anyone was on the ice plateau or at Windy Corner, they were enjoying 50 mph winds or worse. Hot though 11k camp was being up there in that windstorm would be far worse. Even though it was zero degrees at night, the camp turned into a solar oven by the afternoon. With three large walls of ice surrounding the glacier, there was nowhere for the air to go. This geography caused the air temperature to skyrocket.

Later in the day, I thought I heard a bird chirping in camp. Wandering around, I found a black-capped chickadee flitting around the tents. Here was another diminutive songbird far away from the tundra. It disappeared behind a snow wall, chirping a few more times. Then it went silent.

"Strange," I thought. Hoping nothing was wrong with the poor beast, I looked to see if it was injured. Walking around the wall, I was greeted by a surprise. There was nothing there but snow. I walked about, looking to see if it was hiding somewhere. No, it was gone. I heard no chirping or flapping going on. Frowning, I looked into the sky. Had I imagined this flying visitor? I had hallucinated about ravens in Antarctica in my peripheral vision, but I was sure this bird was real.

Yet, it was gone.

"Maybe Alaskan birds have cloaking devices," I teased myself. I thought about asking my neighbors about the bird. Then I thought better of it. There was no need to bother anyone with a trivial question like that. People already looked at me like I was crazy when they heard I was climbing alone. I didn't want to encourage the notion.

I pondered the question of how best to deal with transporting my supplies up to 13.5k camp. How was I going to haul enough emergency supplies in case I was caught in conditions like today without hauling everything? At the minimum, I would need a sleeping bag, shovel, and sleeping pad if I became stuck for a night. But what if a big storm came in, trapping me for several days? Then I would need my stove, fuel, pot, and food.

I didn't want to carry an unnecessary thirty pounds up the mountain. I saw other teams climbing up with fully loaded packs and sleds, then returning completely empty with sleds lashed to their backs like turtle shells. What a joy that must be, to walk with only a liter of water and little else. These climbers were tethered together in a group. Should conditions turn dangerous, they had each other to rely on. Guides likely carried emergency supplies for the group, too.

Last year several people were trapped at Denali Pass at 18,000 feet due to a sick climber. Their guide had to abandon them to get help. This broke the unwritten rule of guiding—never leave your clients. The problem was, he didn't carry a sleeping bag or steel shovel in case they had to bivouac.

I didn't want to end up like them, stuck without shelter and no way to dig a cave. Death was certain in a storm without shelter and a sleeping bag on Denali. As a solo climber, carrying overnight gear was mandatory. The cache run would take six to eight hours. If I wasn't willing to carry the gear to survive a surprise storm, what was I doing here?

Later in the evening, the wind calmed down and quit dragging long tails of snow off Squirrel Point. Snow was still blowing off the cliff, but it looked like the windstorm was dying out. I hoped that tomorrow conditions would be calm enough for a cache run. After a long, hot day at 11k camp, I was ready to move out.

~

When the storm subsides, feelings of discomfort will linger. That's normal and expected—you're human. Don't think of it as weakness. The initial pain of growth gives way to confidence and strength. You'll look back at the challenge you faced and wonder what the big deal was. Remember your struggle and be compassionate with those who are where you once were.

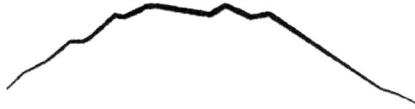

CHAPTER 8

May 14
Lost at Windy Corner

Silence. I awoke to complete quiet. The only sounds that penetrated my mind were my breathing and rustling as I shifted about inside my down feather cocoon. Loosing the bag's draw cord, I twisted my head to hear clearly out of a narrow breathing hole. I listened intently, but all was perfectly still. No sounds emanated from the camp. Even the distant sound of the wind from Squirrel Point was absent.

The day was calm and nothing was going on outside. It was 6:00 a.m., so it was not so surprising that there were no human sounds. What others were doing wasn't my concern, though. It was the wind I was more interested in. If the weather was stable and safe, I would be able to make a cache run to 13.5k camp. My cheeks creased as the beginnings of a smile spread across my face.

Turning my focus inward, I ran through a mental check of how I felt. The headache and general malaise of yesterday were gone. After a full rest day at 11,000 feet, my body had adapted to the thinner atmosphere. I had expected that my training runs to 10,000 feet in Jackson would prevent any bad feelings here. That supposition had been wrong. Now I knew that once I hit 10,000 feet, I had to slow my elevation gain, using the "climb high, sleep low" approach. None of my muscles exhibited any soreness, so my training had paid off.

My stomach growled. Though deep hunger is difficult to wake up to, I welcomed it. Normally I wake up ravenous on expeditions. When I don't feel hungry in the morning, I know altitude or something else is bothering me. This was the ultimate signal that I was ready for more climbing.

I took five minutes to scrape off the built-up frost on the tent's ceiling with a sponge. This morning routine helped put me in motion. Hunger gnawed at me while I got on with it, but I ignored it. The irritation of frost falling down my shirt was more bothersome than an empty stomach. Plus, the sand-sized ice crystals made my down wet, which could lead to greater problems.

Stuffing my head out of the tent door, I looked up Motorcycle Hill. Excitement, nerves, and a cold shiver ran through me. The sun wouldn't peak over the cliff for several hours. I enjoyed the cold and how it affected my body. I knew that with no wind, camp 11k would broil again. I'd rather be scared climbing by myself than baking in stifling heat down here.

I read through Coombs's *Denali's West Buttress* to gauge what I should take and what I should leave. The biggest question I faced was how many days of supplies to bring with me. If I left too much, bad weather at Windy Corner would leave me starving at 11k camp. If I took too little, the second load to 13.5k camp would be too heavy. I brooded about this while shoveling down breakfast, wishing I had butter to add calories to the cereal. If I were with a team, we could bank on stretching out food if we were cut off from our supplies. But by myself, the margin for error was thin.

Begging for food from other climbers was a worst-case scenario. I could make a run down to 10k camp and pull my emergency cache if need be. I didn't want to do that, though. The very idea made me frown and I didn't want to be forced into doing it. This was the first time I realized I might not have the correct mindset for an expedition-style climb. Climbing back and forth was a necessity of climbing Denali. There was no way around it without prior acclimation. I had to climb up and come back down.

After much debating, I decided to leave four days of supplies at 11k camp. Coombs's other recommendation was to take enough gear in case I was caught in a storm. Although the climb was only six hours, I had to be ready for anything. Other teams came down with sleds lashed to empty packs. I knew it was too risky to climb without emergency gear. I had to be able to build a snow cave and sleep in it. That meant carrying a shovel, sleeping bag and pad, stove, fuel, and an extra ration of food.

One climber I spoke with said they were trapped at Windy Corner for three days. I'd be unhappy without food, but dead in three days without water. I didn't want to carry all the extra weight up and down, but I didn't want to be trapped and die from dehydration either. Adding the additional fifteen pounds of safety gear to my pack, I prepared for the first steep climb.

As I clipped on the crampons and yanked the short ice axe out of the snow, I examined Motorcycle Hill. The lower section wasn't that steep, but watching climbers thread their way up the hill yesterday, I knew better than to think this was a quick fifteen-minute walk. Most teams took forty-five to sixty minutes to reach the ridge. The top part took them the longest.

Walking without snowshoes was discomforting. Those were my only protection from falling into a crevasse. If a pit opened up on the hill, I would fall through with crampons. Although I had ice screws, axe, and foot loops, these would only be useful if I wasn't injured or killed. Breaking a bone in a crevasse fall was a worst-case scenario. Whispering a silent prayer for protection, I set off from camp.

When starting off fresh, it is easy to walk too fast and burn out. I knew this, so I settled to a steady, plodding pace. I wanted desperately to go faster but I knew that would be a mistake. I had to save myself for the tougher slopes higher up. As I had left early, I joined two teams climbing the hill. Others had already disappeared and were well on their way up. The timing was perfect. I had the entire slope to myself. On I went, higher and higher.

At first, the climb was relatively easy. But as I neared the top, the sled began tugging at me. I loaded the heaviest items into my pack, with the rest in the orange tub to help alleviate the tension. But still it dragged me backward. Nearing the top, I became nervous. Images of what a slip would do coursed through my mind. I knew such nervousness would wear me out, so I began an out-loud conversation with myself to distract my mind.

"You are doing fine, quit worrying," I said to me.

"It's darned hard not to worry. This isn't an easy climb, you know," I replied to myself.

"Yes, I'm well aware of it. Why did you choose to climb alone?"

"Don't go there. You don't know anyone else who'd go with you on this trip."

"Stay positive. Bemoaning being solo won't improve confidence. That's the whole point of this trip. Look, focus on the next step. See, that was easy."

"It was. Just breathe and stay calm. Focus on the next step and don't look up."

"Right. Good. Worrying about the future is pointless. You can only do what you can do, right now."

I carried on this conversation while making the sweeping left turn to the lip. Sunlight now bathed the slope, illuminating a mass of footprints. The temptation to look up or down was powerful. Looking down brought negative thoughts of being dragged down by my sled. Looking up took energy away, knowing I still had more to climb. Singularly focusing on a left step, then a right step, kept me going. If I stared straight ahead at my foot placement climbing became easier. Deliberate steps were the only way to be safe.

Cresting the top of the hill, I felt simultaneously exhilarated and fearful. I'd made it up the hill, and that bolstered my confidence. The cliff was only twenty feet away. There, before me, was a huge void of air. A massive cliff face farther away provided the backdrop. No breeze broke the stillness. I heard only the distant crunch of another team's crampons far above me.

Walking as close as I dared to the edge, I looked over. The drop must be thousands of feet. To my left, I got a better view of the ridgeline I stood on. All along it was a bulbous serac of rounded ice. Seeing this made me take several steps back. I wanted to be far enough back to avoid snapping off the huge chunk of hardened snow. The view invited a closer look, but I knew better.

Looking toward Squirrel Point, I saw the next obstacle. This portion of the climb was scary. The route followed a chute of ice on the left side of the ridge, offering plenty of protection from wind. But the chute was narrow, at the most twenty feet wide. A slip or a move too far to the left would take me over the cliff. It would be easy to hug the right side, but the danger of rock fall was higher there. Tapping my helmet with the ice axe, I grinned. Motorcycle Hill was, all of the sudden, a child's slope compared to this next ascent. This was going to be much scarier.

Climbing Squirrel Hill

Looking down, I saw several teams climbing up from camp. Today promised to be busy along this portion of the route. There was no time to waste. Due to my caution and a loaded pack, I moved slowly. I didn't want to be the climber causing a traffic jam. I turned and began making my way up the chute. The hill was steep and at first I reveled in the beauty of the icy surface, which sparkled brightly. After a few steps, however, I realized what the sparkle was. The entire chute was covered with chewing gum-sized chipped ice. It was like walking on gravel. Each step I made caused a subtle slip under my foot. If I wasn't dragging a sled, this wouldn't have been a worry, but with a sled full of emergency supplies tugging me backward, the whole experience unnerved me.

Normally, my crampons bit into icy surfaces with pure confidence. The inch-long teeth never slipped and made climbing steep slopes possible. But this slope was different. No matter how hard I stomped, I could not create a secure foothold. It was impossible to force thoughts of the ice breaking away and sliding off the cliff below me out of my mind. I had to build confidence in what I was doing and I needed it right then.

Kneeling down, I took my ice axe and began hacking at the surface with the pick, then the adze. After a couple of swings, I found what I was looking for—solid ice. It was hiding below the crumbly surface, which was just deep enough to make my footing treacherous. In order to gain solid footing, I needed to scrape and kick away the loose shards, then stomp hard into the surface. And I needed to do this for several hundred vertical feet. Sighing, I closed my eyes for a moment, slowly breathing in and out to calm myself.

"This is why you are here, to learn to overcome new challenges," I told myself out loud. I was playing the roles of climber, psychologist, and cheerleader.

"It's not going to be easy. But that's Denali—hard, scary, and impressive," said the shrink.

"You can do it. Step, step, step," shouted the cheerleader.

Opening my eyes, I looked up and felt a mixture of fear and confidence. Now that I knew how to dig to the surface I needed, I felt I could reach the ridge safely. Scraping the Chicklet-style ice away with my axe, there was the solid surface I was looking for. I stood up cautiously, and then I swung my right foot back and kicked into the clear spot. Crunch. My crampon stuck fast. Twisting my foot left and right, there was no give. This was the surface I needed to climb the chute to Squirrel Point in safety.

When climbing with crampons, I normally just stomp hard and my boots stick. With this loose ice, that just didn't work. Stomping merely packed ice into my crampons and made my footing worse. Now all I needed to do was paw at the loose stuff until I felt resistance, then kick. Each pawing motion with my foot sounded like a metal spatula dragging through broken glass. Dozens of little shards tinkled down the slope with each kick. The slope was steep enough to require me to use my ice axe as a cane for balance.

Slowly, oh so slowly, I worked my way up. A single spot, halfway up the hill, allowed for the only rest. After the continual noise of cracked ice sloughing down the chute, the sound of my pursed breathing sounded remarkably loud. Although I saw teams top out on Motorcycle Hill, their voices were eaten by the vast space around us.

I stood and focused on breathing. Phew, phew, phew. It was time to move. Although the chute was a short climb, the exposure ate my energy. Focusing on the slope in front of me and not looking up nor down took all of my concentration. Every time I looked up, my energy flagged. My brain told me the top was too far away. I knew this slope was not technically difficult; it was only tough. When crossing Antarctica, I learned that focusing too far ahead was disheartening and sapped energy. Once I knew my goal and which way to go, I just had to keep my eyes on the next step only. The slope was steep enough to feel like it was in my face, so all I had to do was concentrate on staring straight ahead, perform my paw and kick maneuver, and move up.

It wasn't long before I reached the top. As soon as my sled stopped pulling me backward, I stopped. With my hands on my knees and eyes closed to take a breather, I let the fear and anxiety flow over me. When I had enough, I stood straight up and visualized a mental picture of the emotions slipping off me like shower water, dripping onto the snow and out of my mind. Opening my eyes, I forced a smile, did a fist pump, and exhaled a heartfelt "Yeah!"

Looking out across the plateau, I saw the first flat pan of ice I'd seen since arriving on Denali. There was a small ridge to walk on. It split the difference between two dangers. On the left was a towering rock face. I could hear small rocks clattering down the thousands of feet every few minutes, so I tightened my helmet's chinstrap. On the right the ice ended in a sheer cliff. With clear skies, either was easy to avoid. A half-dozen wands marked the trail across the blue ice. It was a joy to walk across it and the easiest bit of travel thus far. That was, until I felt the sun's heat.

With no breeze, the sun's rays toasted me from all directions. Dragging the sled made it feel as hot as the Mojave Desert in August. Although the walk was flat, hard, and easy, the heat in the air cancelled out those advantages. I stopped and stripped down to my light wool shirt.

A half-mile away, near Windy Corner, I could see multiple teams at work. Some were moving up the hill; others appeared to be working cache holes. A few were taking a break. I was surprised at how many teams had climbed well ahead of me. I didn't hear them at all in the morning, even though they must have walked within ten feet of my tent.

As I approached the base of the hill, the air grew hotter by the minute. What should have been a simple walk turned into a trudge through an inferno. The mixture of heat and the looming slope sapped my energy. By the time I reached the base of the hill, my legs had powered down. I simply stopped and looked up. It was 1:00 p.m. Though the air wasn't as hot as it had been at 11k camp, the sun's radiation beat on my head.

A two-person team left their cache hole and headed toward me.

"Hi there," I called out.

"Hello, how are you?" the man replied.

"Great, except for the heat. This is surreal."

"It takes some getting used to. You're welcome to use our cache hole if you like."

"Thank you. Did you summit?"

"No, we were stuck here three days in a wind storm. My daughter and I had to take shelter. We're headed back down."

"You stayed up here the whole time?" I asked.

"Yes, it wasn't pleasant. We're from Alaska but this was extra tough."

I couldn't believe it. A couple I knew once told me they made the exact same mistake by doing the one thing their guide book had warned them against. A plateau looks like a wonderful camp. Don't be fooled. It's the worst place to get stuck in a storm.

"I hope you weren't injured? Do you need anything?"

"No, thank you. We're fine."

The man turned to his daughter, nodded, and clipped in his safety rope.

"Have a good climb," he said. "Watch out for those crevasses around Windy Corner."

"Thanks for the warning. Be safe!"

He started down from the base of the hill, toward the plateau. His daughter followed after him, keeping the rope between them. Too little slack and she'd yank him backward. Too much and she'd be stomping on the line with crampons, risking damage to their crevasse protection.

As they moved away across the plateau, other teams advanced on my position. Feeling fatigued from the sun, I stood looking at the hole, debating what to do. Up the slope, others continued to work their caches. I wanted to bury my supplies and head back down. But I knew that would leave me with an awkward haul when I advanced to 13.5k camp. Would I pick up my cache and single-haul it with the rest? Or should I tough it out to 13.5k camp, bury my cache, and return to 11k? Even though it was uncomfortably warm here, I dreaded to think of the solar oven called 11k camp. That was worse.

While I debated, teams continued to pass me up the hill. Some climbers smiled and said "Hello!" with enthusiasm. Others completely ignored me, focusing instead on keeping their feet moving. Then a military team came by. They were chatty and jovial, even though their loads were huge.

"You guys must be pretty tough to haul that kind of load," I said, trying to keep it humorous.

"Sure, these are heavy, but it's still nothing compared to what we normally carry in combat," laughed the sergeant. "You should see those packs."

"I have no doubt. At least no one is shooting at you here."

"True. It's a toss-up between altitude or bullets."

A second military team came up behind the first and stopped. The sergeant asked if I'd like to rope in to go around the crevasse field.

"That's nice of you, thanks. I'm not traveling very fast."

"We're not exactly burning up the hill ourselves."

"Sure, I'll join. I appreciate it. Falling in a crevasse isn't my idea of a fun day."

Pointing to the third of four men, the staff sergeant said, "John will let some line out and tie you in."

The team moved up thirty feet until I was at the correct rope position. Clipping in, I thought, "So much for climbing Denali solo. But it's no good if I end up trapped in a hole. Better to return alive."

As soon as I nodded the team began moving on up. It took nearly an hour to reach the saddle at Windy Corner. My speed matched theirs until the end when the sergeant sped up. "The horse smelling the barn," I thought. We took a short water and pee break, then prepared to move up the hill and around Windy Corner. As we started out, a large bank of clouds blew up out of the valley toward us. Soon, a thick soup was upon us, reducing visibility to fifty yards.

I was glad to be clipped in, as the dangerous slope at Windy Corner was steep. Every step I took made my sled swing toward the cliff, violently yanking me back and forth. The rest of my rope team only had backpacks, so they moved with relative ease.

"Sorry, guys, could you slow it just a half-click? This sled is killing me."

Nodding, the staff sergeant slowed down for a bit, but soon resumed his pace. It felt like they were trying to make the best time possible before a complete whiteout enveloped us. Soon, we reached the crevasses. True to Special Forces fashion, the team marched over the crevasse without even slowing down. It made sense, as standing around in a crevasse field is a bad idea. My sled dipped to the side a bit but didn't slip into any of the three crevasses we crossed.

In another ten minutes we arrived at 13.5k camp, in a complete whiteout. The military guys and gals floated in a milky fog. We stumbled in the soft snow from speed and fatigue.

I unclipped and coiled the line. "Thanks for the line around Windy Corner. I now see what you mean by the danger there."

"Sure thing. It's a pretty hairy place. Are you going to be okay going back by yourself?"

"Yeah, I think so. There's a trail to follow. Once I unload my sled, it'll be an easier walk."

Bumping gloves like boxers (it was too cold to take them off for a proper handshake), the staff sergeant returned to his team and began setting up camp. It was impossible to see a good location for a cache. I knew if I wandered too far down the slope, there were building-sized crevasses. I decided to stay fifty feet away from the military tent and dug the hole. It took much longer to dig it, place the supplies, and fill it back up in the thinner atmosphere. In Jackson at 6,000 feet, I could've finished the job in ten minutes. Here it took nearly half an hour. I could only shovel ten loads before I had to stand up and take a breather. Each time, I was light-headed.

"Welcome to altitude," I told myself.

There was no reason to hang out. It was 3:00 p.m. and the light breeze wasn't clearing the clouds. In fact, they seemed to grow thicker. Quickly lashing the empty sled to my pack, I prepared to leave. Somehow my pack felt like it still weighed forty pounds. A solo climb, with extra safety gear, is never easy. I was jealous of the other teams climbing down the mountain with empty packs and sleds.

Waving to the military team, I set off back down the trail. In a minute, they disappeared.

"Grunts in the mist," I said, laughing to myself.

At first, it was easy to follow the trail in the soft snow. Once I reached the crevasses, however, I was in a whiteout. The crevasses were still visible, just about. The jagged holes were hazy white on the edges, light blue then deep blue down their sides, and utterly black in the middle. All at once I wondered what I was doing here. The irregular voids mesmerized me. Letting out a slow whistle, I broke the trance and leapt over each in turn, stopping to take a breath. Each hop increased my heart rate. I wasn't sure if it was the effort or the fear. Probably both.

As I rounded Windy Corner, I heard small rocks crack into the slope somewhere above my head. Checking the fit of my helmet, I prayed none would hit me. A fist-sized rock falling a thousand feet is more than adequate to kill anyone.

The trail quickly disappeared on the hard ice, leaving me in a haze of white. It was completely impossible to see where to go. Stooping over and looking at the ice, I barely made out crampon tracks. In a few minutes, however, they too disappeared. After standing for a minute and scanning around me, I found one more broken wand. Then the trail utterly vanished and I wasn't sure which way to go.

I kept at the same elevation and rounded the corner, still looking for the trail. I was careful not to lose sight of the broken wand. The ice was as hard as concrete and I made no footprints. Even though I could kick in toe marks, they were invisible in the whiteout. I walked back and forth to the last wand several times, trying to find the trail. No luck.

"Great crud!" I muttered.

I was lost.

"Hello, is anyone out there?" I yelled.

No response. Only a light wind swirling in the fog, with me floating in it. After several minutes of examining the ground, I thought I found a trail. It moved up and to the right. I followed it. After a few minutes of walking, I found myself on a steep slope, steeper than it should be. With each step, the ice cracked and slipped down the hill. This wasn't good. I didn't remember any of this when coming up.

I was lost on Windy Corner.

"This can't be right," I told myself. "Those couldn't have been tracks. Your eyes and brain are playing tricks on you."

Backtracking, I retreated fifty feet from the slope, following my trail of broken snow sheets. My mind raced for a solution. Being completely blind and lost in the clouds, there was no way I could find the trail. The compass around my neck wouldn't help me. My GPS didn't have a track to follow.

"Wait, my GPS!" I exclaimed.

Right before I left for Alaska, I uploaded a few waypoints onto my Garmin GPS. I only put in the major ones, but hopefully they included a point for the saddle so that I might make it back. Once there, the soft snow trail would be easy to follow. I powered the unit up and waited anxiously. The screen silently displayed its parade of power-up screens.

```
Garmin GPS
[legal info]
Initializing GPS.
Downloading waypoints and tracks.
Finding satellites...
```

What normally took a few seconds seemed to take minutes. Even though I wasn't moving and the slope wasn't breaking away under my feet anymore, I could taste the fear of being lost.

```
63° 04.093N 151° 06.541W
```

Clicking on the map, I zoomed in until I found the nearest waypoint. My eyes lit up. The marker description indicated the saddle at the base of Windy Corner. I clicked on the marker. It was the exact waypoint I needed.

And it was a quarter mile away.

I was way off-route. I visualized the trail as I remembered going up it. I was literally on the cliff face. Should I have gone any farther, the entire face might have broken off, sliding down the mountain and taking me with it. I couldn't believe how quickly I'd walked off the trail. My heart raced. I had to get off this slope and get back to it.

Turning downhill, I stomped as quickly as my clown boots and crampons allowed. It took several moments before the GPS stabilized. I had to move far enough for the tracking indicator to show my direction of travel. If I walked too far in the wrong direction before it locked in, I could still fall into an invisible void. The only thing I could see was the little unit in my hand. There was nothing else visible through my goggles but gray-white. My respiration increased and I fought to control the rising fear. Being lost on Windy Corner was a worst-case scenario. There were crevasses, huge and small, all around me. Should I fall in, no one would know.

After what seemed forever, the direction pointer stabilized and turned toward the waypoint. This was the fastest quarter mile I'd covered on the entire trip. Within one hundred feet of the waypoint, I barely discerned a bamboo wand. I was saved. Slowing down, I found the trail. After another moment of hurried walking, I arrived at the saddle.

"Whoo-hoo!" I cried out. "That was way too close."

While nearly jogging to my waypoint, the GPS tracked my route. Zooming in on the map, I saw that I had indeed nearly walked off the cliff. For the second time in an afternoon, I questioned what I was doing here. Now I understood the challenge Lone Dupre, the first January Denali soloist, faced. He was blinded by whiteouts and darkness. Becoming lost here could prove fatal in just a few steps.

Now that I was on the saddle in soft snow, the trail was easy to discern. I knew I would have trouble on the hard ice plateau, but there would be more marks of human passage to help me: pee stains. The wind couldn't remove those from the blue ice.

Although I was blinded, I had little trouble making my way down the hill. Once on the blue plateau, my pulse rate slowed and I walked in silence. Following the combination of broken wands, crampon tracks, and pee stains, I made my way toward Squirrel Point.

All of the sudden, I heard a grinding sound behind me. Whipping around, I saw a gray form coming right at me. I sucked in my breath in panic.

"What the…?"

All at once, I realized it was a skier. He slid past me to a stop.

"Dude, you scared the crud out of me! What's your name?"

"Tony. Sorry, I'm trying to get out of the whiteout and down the hill. My partners are behind me. What's yours?" Tony replied in Australian-accented English.

I told him as I relaxed.

"How in the world did you find your way down?" I asked. "I got lost up there."

"It wasn't easy but I followed my GPS track."

"I wish I'd made one. It would've saved me from almost walking off the cliff."

"No kidding! Good thing you didn't."

"Hah! You're telling me. You have two friends behind you?"

"Yes, they're much slower. They're walking down. I left them at the saddle as the trail was obvious."

We chatted a little bit more about the climbing, the conditions, and what each of us was doing. It was nearly the same conversation I had with everyone else. After our banter petered out, Tony excused himself as he wanted to get down the chute and out of the whiteout.

"That's a pretty narrow chute for skis. I'll bet it's exciting."

"It's actually not too bad going down, but the exposure is big," he replied.

Smiling, he turned and made his way to the crossed wands at the crest of Squirrel Point. He stopped, turned to look back for a moment, and then disappeared over the lip.

"That guy is a powerhouse," I thought. "I wish I was a solid downhill skier. Sliding downhill beats walking down any day."

Arriving at the edge of the plateau, I expected to be scared at the steepness. It was almost a disappointment. For some reason, the slope didn't look nearly as steep as when I had climbed it that morning. It was no steeper, in fact than Mt. Glory in Jackson. All at once, I was relieved. Although I had to be careful, holding my ice axe in case of a fall, I felt no fear. It was only a steep walk down. I saw Tony at the top of Motorcycle Hill, waiting at the end of the chute. After two hours of frowning, I cracked a smile and held it all the way down the slope.

At the bottom, next to Tony, I looked back and saw his two climbing partners emerge out of the clouds, as though they were floating. What a view. Then I excused myself from Tony and continued on down towards 11k camp. I didn't want to risk ending up on the serac on the cliff because I was unable to see where I was walking.

Arriving in camp at 5:00 p.m., I plopped down in the snow, chugging water. The heat of the upper climb had taken it out of me. Adrenaline had fueled my decent. Now, its magic had worn off, leaving me fatigued. I waited and watched for Tony's teammates to make the crest of the hill and start down.

Retreating into my tent, I rested for an hour. The air down here was still hot, and I didn't want to be in the sun. Although I was hungry, I ate unenthusiastically. The effort of caching had taken a lot out of me, and thinking about how I'd wandered onto the crumbling cliff disturbed my emotions, consuming yet more energy. Close calls were the things I disliked the most. Bad weather didn't bother me, but losing the trail was a whole other matter.

It took some time after eating before I felt better. My thoughts wandered back to my training. I had only spent one twelve-hour day towing a sled up and down a mountain. Though it had been tough, it hadn't been scary. I realized now that my training hadn't been adequate psychologically. I needed to have somehow integrated fear into it. I needed to build up my resilience to adrenaline's parching effect, which meant a huge rush followed by a massive crash.

There was nothing I could do about that now. I told myself to focus. Not wanting to burn myself out, I decided that tomorrow I'd take a recovery day. I needed to get myself back in a more positive frame of mind before moving up.

~

There may be dangers lurking in places where you don't expect them. If you're unsure of yourself, return to your plan, even though it may have changed from the original. Return to your last known location and try again.

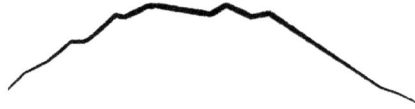

Chapter 9

May 15
Sauna

Today I woke up at 7:00 a.m., much later than usual. The drama of yesterday had sapped my energy, leaving me lethargic and unexcited. I was taking a rest day, so I stayed in the sleeping bag and wrote in my journal about the previous day's events.

Writing about how I had become lost took more energy than I thought it would. When I had rough days in Antarctica, I was slow at writing. Reliving the experience made me feel the rush of adrenaline all over again. But then I had limited time to capture the experience on paper. Now I had all day and was in no rush.

Looking up at Squirrel Point, I saw no snow blowing off the cliff. In fact, everything was quite dead. A few teams moved out after an 8:00 a.m. breakfast. After that, things grew quiet. As soon as the sun rose over the mountain, the temperature began to rise. It was going to be a long, hot day.

As I didn't need my snowshoes higher on the mountain, I decided to cache them before the day became too hot. I debated about where to build the cache. I probed around with my trekking poles to find relatively soft snow; I didn't want to dig a foot down only to encounter a hard layer of ice. Energy conservation was a high priority and it was important not to waste effort smashing through the ice with my steel shovel. After some searching around my tent, I found an ideal spot and set to digging.

Snowshoes are quite long. Several times I thought I had shoveled enough and test-fitted the shoes, but they still stuck far out above the hole I had made. I thought about cutting the hole wider and laying the snowshoes flat, but I was concerned about the snow melting and losing them. Other teams' caches of skis and supplies had melted out and were almost falling over. I wanted to ensure that my gear stayed put and didn't disappear. Eventually, I had to jump in the hole and keep digging until it was deep enough.

The hole allowed me to cache my first week of garbage as well. There was no reason to haul one more ounce up the mountain than necessary. Scrounging through my gear, I rooted out every pouch, scrap, and anything else I knew I wouldn't need higher on the mountain. After some searching, I cobbled together an extra pound to leave behind. It doesn't seem like much, but every pound feels like five at 14,000 feet.

At noon, I felt better and wandered camp. I wanted to remain active to stay in shape. Lying and sitting around all day was a recipe for becoming weaker. Motivating myself was difficult as the temperature rose, but I knew inaction was worse.

A few people milled about, minding their own business. Those who weren't preparing to climb were standing and chatting. There were all varieties of tents, in a rainbow of colors. Quite a few were from Hilleberg, the same maker as mine. Some had North Face, Mountain Hardware, and assorted other brands.

One tent caught my eye. It was green-tan, but that wasn't what drew my attention. It was covered in writing. Striding through the snow to get a closer look, I began to read what it said. Instantly, I roared with laughter. Across the side of the tent, in broad Sharpie, were the words "The Crazy Fart Castle." Someone had finally fessed up to the results of digestive joy from the wretched diets climbers enjoyed. Other entertaining phrases were scrawled in smaller handwriting.

Laughing all the way back to my tent, I thought about all the stomach-churning meals I've enjoyed over the years. I've learned to avoid many of them, as the gastrointestinal turbulence they can create makes life in a remote location tougher than it already is.

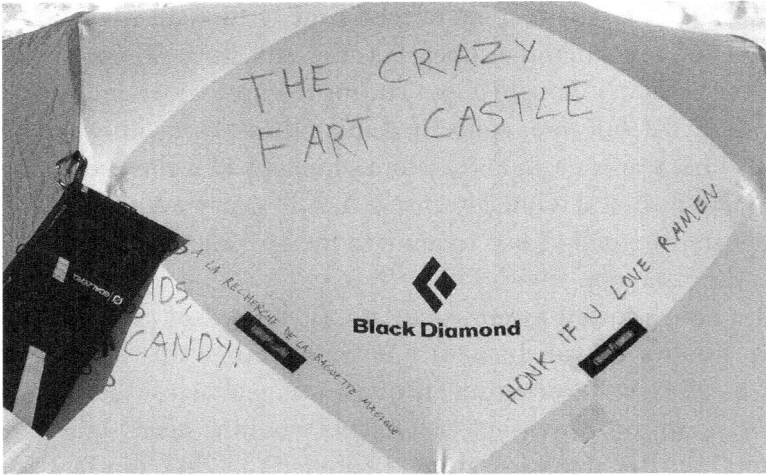

By 2:00 p.m., the air was 90°. I slathered on another layer of sunscreen as I felt the sun's radiation sizzling my skin. All I could do was sit facing away from the sun, looking at Motorcycle Hill. I couldn't believe how hot it was, even with thin cloud cover. Flipping up the collar of my white hiking shirt, I tilted my hat back, trying to cut out any direct contact from the sun. It still wasn't enough.

I hopped into the tent for a bit, hoping somehow that it would be cooler. It wasn't. The air inside was stifling and felt fifteen degrees hotter. I couldn't believe the heat, being in the middle of Alaska on a thousand-foot-thick block of ice. It felt like Las Vegas in summer, minus the casinos.

After pondering it out, I decided I needed a stronger sun shield. Looking at my options, I settled on the sled. The plastic was thick and should block out all of the sun's direct rays. Digging a small hole, I jammed the sled into the snow and hid behind it. The relief was only marginal. I couldn't believe it. The nearly 360° wall of thousand-foot-high ice made the sun feel like it came from every direction.

I removed my shirt and stuffed the hiking poles into the sleeves. Propping it up like a scarecrow behind me, I felt a little better. Still, it was barely tolerable. Sitting on my poop can, I maneuvered the sled and shirt until I had an open-air sun shield. If I shifted six inches left or right, the sunlight seared my skin. The fumes from the poop can were unpleasant, but it was better than being barbecued.

For the next three hours, I sat, drank water, nibbled food, and did nothing else. Looking around camp, everyone else was doing what they could do to cope. Several climbing teams were walking around shirtless and rubbing snow on themselves. I copied their idea and did the same. Stripping my shirt, I grabbed handfuls of icy snow and rubbed it all over my chest and back. The stinging cold was a welcome diversion from the scorching air. However, it felt like rubbing myself with broken glass.

Brutal as it was, I was having fun. The challenge of obtaining a degree of comfort kept me busy during an otherwise do-nothing day. I looked at the massive ice chunks above camp and wondered if they'd break off in the heat and squash us all. Pushing the thought from my mind, I refocused on telling myself I was enjoying myself.

Avoiding the death spiral of negativity as a result of unpleasant conditions was crucial. If I focused on the tough parts, it would be difficult to concentrate on safely reaching the summit. A minor negative distraction is all it takes on a steep, treacherous mountain to die.

At 5:00 p.m., the glacier violently shuddering raised me out of my stupor. Two seconds later, a spectacular rumble of thunder permeated the pocket valley.

"What happened?" I called out to no one in particular.

Climbers were looking up and around. Nothing appeared to be happening. Had a massive serac broken off, causing the glacier to shift? There was no way to tell. As the rumble dissipated, I looked up again at the ice above camp.

"I sure hope those chunks don't fall off. That'd be the biggest death toll on Denali ever."

It was impossible to ignore thoughts of earthquakes, broken ice, and avalanches. Other climbers were similarly jarred out of their stupor and were talking with each other about what had taken place. No one seemed to know what it was for sure, as I found out when I asked one group of climbers what they thought it could be.

"I don't know what that was. All we know was that our thermometers hit one hundred and five degrees today. We couldn't move."

"One hundred and five? That's insane! I've got to move up out of here."

"Yes, we're leaving this evening to get out of the heat."

"I don't blame you. I'm headed up early tomorrow. I don't want to do another one of these days."

Far above, three birds flitted about and played aerial tag with each other. This was the third time I had seen birds so many miles from the forest. I couldn't believe they flew this far to play in the thermals. I wished I could be up there with them in the cooling breezes, unafraid of falls.

The rest of the evening was uneventful, with no more earthquakes. I packed what I could so I was ready to go early the next day. I wanted to make the top of the plateau before the sun hit at 9:00 a.m. Even if there were strong winds, I was leaving 11k camp and heading up, no matter what. I had no desire to roast and dehydrate another day.

∽

The long grind will sap your spirit. Do what is necessary to keep yourself going despite the discomfort. Find something to focus on to positively buoy your attitude.

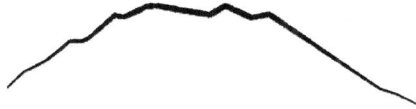

CHAPTER 10

May 16
11k to 13.2k camp

Silence surrounded camp 11k when I awoke in my tent the following morning. The only sound was from me rustling the waterproof nylon of my teal-colored sleeping bag. The sound of falling snow was conspicuously absent. Excited to see how conditions were on Squirrel Hill, I wriggled around like a massive slug, unzipped the top tent door, and peered up.

Nothing moved under a grayish blue sky. The outline of Squirrel Point was perfect, as though a child had roughly carved out the mountain with scissors. Sleep drained from me and my eyes opened fully wide.

All the tents in the camp were coated in four inches of snow. I remembered waking up to the sound of the tick-tick-tick of falling snow landing on my tent during the night. The sound of snow, something so minute, was surprisingly loud in the absence of all other noise. It sounded as though someone was tapping on the nylon with sewing needles.

It was time. Here was my chance to move up the mountain in perfect weather. After the crushing heat of yesterday, I wanted to escape. I shook my head at the thought of staying another day inside the solar oven of camp 11k.

"No way," I told myself. "I'm outta here."

Grabbing the food mug, I scraped the frost off the ceiling. Chunks were already missing where I had rubbed against the tent while looking outside. The Western Mountaineering Puma bag was waterproof, so I wasn't worried about it. With my excitement building, I didn't care that my tousled hair was now full of frost. Leaning my head sideways like I was clearing water, I scrubbed the ice out of my hair while leaning outside.

"No point getting more ice inside the tent than there already is," I said. "I want to get moving. There's no way I want to hit that pig of a hill at Windy Corner at 1:00 p.m. again."

I curled my lip at the thought of standing on the glacial plateau, nauseous from the broiling heat. Avoiding the heat motivated me into action, though it was only 5:00 a.m. I wanted to move out of camp and start climbing before 8:00 a.m. Plus, I only had four days of rations left down here. If a large storm moved in, I would be separated from my rations 2,500 feet above me. Four days of food may sound adequate but on Denali a storm can easily last that long. Plus, it took a half-day's worth of food to climb to my depot. In effect, I only had three days of food. Being stuck for three days was routine. I wanted none of that at 11k camp.

There were a lot of things to do, the first of which was eating breakfast. Though the air was a cold -10°F, it felt too warm to me. It should have felt far colder. I knew today was going to be another hot one.

After chowing down breakfast, I packed my gear. I planned to leave nothing behind, aside from my snowshoes and trash. All I had to do was pile my gear into the sled and backpack. The experience of two days previously had taught me I needed to load my pack up as heavy as I could stand. Having too much weight inside the sled made climbing scary. With no backup, a simple trip was potentially fatal. I wanted to focus on staying alive, so I packed the densest items deep inside my pack: shovels, stove, fuel, electronics, and food.

Once I had packed everything, I hopped out and looked around. Only a few campers stirred, preparing for whatever they were going to do today. Motorcycle Hill was already covered in boot prints, so other teams must have started out at night after the snow fell. Seeing that track boosted my confidence. Knowing someone had walked through meant there was little chance of a crevasse opening up before I surmounted the hill.

I quietly whistled a random string of notes while breaking down the tent. I felt alive and excited to be moving again. Spending several days in a camp made me feel lazy, like I wasn't strong enough to forge on. I knew that my feelings didn't match the logic of high-altitude climbing. Staying at a location, climbing up, and then dropping back down to sleep were absolutely necessary. Still, I couldn't ignore the feeling.

My last duty before heading uphill was to dispose of the poop bag. It had been a full week since I'd arrived on Denali and the can was heavy and full. I didn't want to haul waste up a mountain. I cared about ounces and the can was full of pounds. Powerful fumes assailed my nostrils as I opened the can with ungloved hands.

"Whoa," I gagged. "That's wretched."

Carefully pulling the plastic bag out, I knotted the top and marched fifty feet over to the official poop crevasse. The gash in the middle of camp looked innocuous and unthreatening but I knew better. The rangers had selected this crevasse because it was deep and the sides steep. Escape from it would be impossible by myself.

The camp was still silent. No stoves roared. Though a few climbers milled about, none made any noise, the fresh snow dampening all of their movements. Even the "ziff-ziff" sound of their nylon clothing was inaudible.

Standing as close to the crevasse as I dared, I swung back the bag and then heaved it forward. The clear bag filled with waste sailed through the air. It hit the edge of the crevasse with a dull thump, and then slipped into the hole. I stared and started counting off the seconds. I wanted to estimate how deep it was.

I counted to nine out loud. My eyes bulged out. I never even heard the thud-boom of the bag striking the bottom of the crevasse. Not even a splat, plop, or crack echoed up from the slash in the snow.

"How deep is this thing?" I wondered aloud. All at once I found myself slowly backing away from the hole, a peculiar fear rising inside of me. That bag was easily five pounds and should have made some noise, yet nothing ever came out of the crack in the glacier. It was as though the sound was trapped in it, rather like how a black hole in space traps light—nothing escapes.

Safely a full ten feet from the hole, I peered into it once more. If this small gash was essentially bottomless, how deep were the larger crevasses in this glacier? Visions of a network of cracks opening up all around filled my mind. I conjured up a picture of a crevasse opening up under my tent and swallowing my entire camp.

I played the whole scenario out in my mind. I had read about others having crevasses open up right next to their tents. It had happened to other climbers. Exactly why crevasses should open up at night was a mystery to me. I understood them opening in daylight when the sun's heat melted the snow, but at night when it was cold…? Whatever the answer to the mystery was, I had no desire to observe it happening under me. The silent lack of a boom from the poop crevasse hinted at the real danger of glacial travel.

For a moment, my mind went wild, filling me with fear. I imagined that an earthquake had broken the glacier loose. It was now ready to slide and take the climbing camp with it. My imaginings were becoming too vivid. It was time to move up the mountain.

I hoisted and clipped in my pack. Pulling the sled out of camp, I lined myself up in the existing tracks. Far up on the hill were visible crevasses, some marked with crossed wands. I knew there must be others lurking around. I was glad the sky was clear so I didn't wander off course.

I smiled as I yelled, "Yo!" and felt like John Wayne leading a wagon train out. Upward I went.

The deeper snow from last night's fall made the climb slower and more challenging than last time. Though it also made dragging the sled uphill tougher, it did, however, mean that the sled stuck better when I stopped for a breather. Wriggling the trace lines around, I was able to wedge the sled into the packed freshly fallen snow so I didn't have to dig a posthole to secure it with. I don't enjoy post-holing so I was pleased that the soft snow prevented the sled from sliding backward. It more than made up for the extra effort of pulling it.

Ascending the hill slowly, I looked back repeatedly and enjoyed the view all the way up. My progress was halting but I didn't mind. I wasn't going anywhere but up. This time I reveled in the sights of the camp as I rose above it. Then I looked over the glacier below the camp. The air was clear and cold. I could see what seemed thirty miles down Kahiltna Glacier. The view filled me with energy. This was why I was here.

Cresting Motorcycle Hill in seventy-five minutes, I stopped for a snack. My plan was to move as quickly as I could up the hill. The higher I was when the sun appeared, the happier I would be. Looking down to 11k camp, I felt like the lord of a vast kingdom. Though I knew I was but an ant, the landscape made me feel grand. I was alive and having a majestic time.

The mountain above me started glowing. I knew the sun would soon peek over it. I ate my dry granola bar and started up Squirrel Hill chute. Instead of Chicklet-sized cracked ice, the path was coated in snow.

"This should be entertaining," I said.

Taking a first few tentative steps, I stomped hard to feel the surface. There was hard-packed ice immediately below the soft fluff. The texture of the ice had changed completely from when I had climbed the route two days ago. Hard and unyielding, my crampons bit into the ice and held fast. There was not enough snow to worry about an avalanche, though the thought crossed my mind.

"Stop thinking so much. You're too much inside your head. Focus outside and pay attention," I muttered. If I disappeared inside my imagination too much, I would lose both focus and my footing. I concentrated on each step, the steep slope in my face.

Stomp and crunch. The sound of my crampon-laden boots did wonders for my confidence. Behind me, my sled made a "shish-shish" sound. Slowly, ever so slowly, I moved up the mountain.

At the halfway mark up the chute, the sun peeked over the mountain.

"Dang!" I hissed. I had hoped to be all the way to Squirrel Point before the sun peeked over the mountain. Looking up the chute, I found myself staring straight into it. At first, I tried to continue climbing without my glasses, as I didn't want to stop. After five minutes of squinting, however, I had to put them on. If the sun were on the horizon, I could tough it out for an hour, but it was already high in the sky and growing more intense every minute. I dreaded developing snow blindness.

Turning around, I wrapped the sled trace around my knee to hold my position. It was somewhat precarious, but there was no other way to unzip my pocket and still be ready with the ice axe should I slip. After a few anxious moments, I extricated the glasses and slipped them onto my face, through my greasy hair.

Facing back uphill, I grinned. The sun no longer blinded me. I enjoyed the sunlight raking across the rough snow. The low angle of the light made the snow stand out in stunning relief. I had already become too hot in the few minutes I had been in the sunlight so I unzipped my jacket. It made no difference. I would have to remove it.

I thought about pushing through, climbing the rest of the way and putting up with the sweating. But I knew I would feel nauseous at the top of the hill if I did that. It was a dumb move to stop and remove my jacket. Other climbers would probably tough it out, but overheating was worse for me. I had to remove the jacket, with my pack on, all the while standing on this precipitous slope. I had practiced this maneuver plenty of times on Glory Mountain in Jackson, but I had never done it with a fifty-pound sled pulling me into a void as it threatened to now.

Silently cursing myself for not taking my jacket off at the bottom of the chute and momentarily freezing, I began the process. Loosening one shoulder strap, I withdrew my arm. The pack slipped around my waist, pulling me to the side. Breathing in and out slowly to control my fear, I fought to free my arm. This was the most delicate part of the operation. With my right arm wedged in the jacket, I was helpless. Though I held the ice axe in my left hand in the event of a fall, the jacket would prove a straitjacket. I wouldn't be able to maneuver.

"Stay calm. Follow the procedure. Concentrate on what you're doing," I repeated out loud.

After several failures, I finally popped my arm out. The sled hadn't moved.

"Whew!" I breathed as I pulled on the right backpack strap. I strapped the ice axe back on my right hand and yanked the jacket out through the whole mess of straps. I was free and feeling cooler already.

"Let's not do that again," I said.

"Yah, no kidding, dufus," I replied.

Talking through both sides of the conversation focused my thinking. It helped me feel like I had a mentor with me, correcting my mistakes.

Soon, I topped out on the huge ice plateau. I had made it up again without incident. Elated, I began hiking across the ice. Halfway to what I called Pig Hill, I looked down a canyon to the right. A building-sized block of ice lay smashed across the glacier. Car-sized chunks surrounded the huge monolith. Marveling at it for a minute, I put together what happened.

When the earthquake hit, everything on the mountain shook. Being so short in duration, the earthquake shouldn't have made any noise. Yet a few seconds after, a tremendous boom had resounded through 11k camp. I now knew what had caused it. That chunk of ice was several hundred feet tall. I couldn't believe how big it was and how easily it had broken away from the mountain. Then I thought about the big seracs dangling over 11k camp. What if those broke loose?

By the time I reached the base of Pig Hill, a cold breeze had picked up. It was from the sun warming the air. It was cold enough to burn my skin and make me shiver. I desperately wanted to put my jacket back on but I knew I couldn't. If I did, I would end up having to remove it again on the climb, just like on Squirrel Point.

"No way. Tough it out! Come on, it'll only be a few minutes and you'll be toasty," I told myself.

Sure enough, after climbing for five minutes, I overheated and had to roll up my sleeves. Though the air was 15°F, I was struggling to stay cool. When flushes of heat flowed through me, my skin warmed up. When they stopped, my arms felt like they were in an icy pond. The sensation was absurd, alternating between too hot and too cold. I regulated my step speed to keep from overheating or freezing.

After an hour, I reached the saddle at Windy Corner. I had finished off the toughest part of the vertical climb. Now I had to negotiate the cliff and the crevasses. As I moved around the corner, my sled slid toward the cliff. This time, being heavier, it didn't swing back and forth, yanking me off my feet. I couldn't believe I was actually happy to have extra weight.

After I had made my way around Windy Corner, I encountered a split in the trail. Now, instead of one way across to the crevasses, there were two paths. One went higher up, over what looked to be a thicker snow bridge. The other was the path I'd used two days ago. Confident with what I had done before, I leapt over each of the two crevasses, then pulled my sled across. Compared to my experience a few days ago, it felt effortless.

I arrived at 13.5k camp at 2:00 p.m. With a cheer, I plopped onto the sled and relaxed. I had made it. I dug out my cache and prepared camp.

I thought about continuing on to 14k camp but remembered the warning in Coombs's *Denali's West Buttress* book. It said that some teams had been permanently wiped out pushing past 13.5k camp. I had time, supplies, and I felt good; there was no reason to push forward and risk altitude sickness. Instead, I opted to build my camp and enjoy the scenery. The city-block sized crevasses below 13.5k camp were awe-inspiring.

Later in the day, a Japanese couple climbed up and settled into 13.5k camp in the pit dug by the military team. We chatted for a while about their climb, what they were planning to do, and how they felt. Nori did all the talking for the team, as I guessed his wife spoke little or no English. His was heavily accented but understandable. They made for pleasant campmates.

Over the course of the rest of the day and evening, a few teams climbed past toward 14k camp. Enjoying the view and relaxation helped drain the stress of solo climbing. I smiled and appreciated the grand views.

∽

Don't be discouraged if you have to take smaller steps than you planned. Small movements forward are still movement.

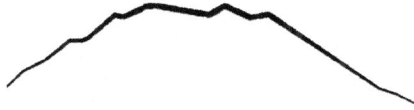

Chapter 11

May 17
Move from Camp 13.2k to 14.2k
Japanese team

I woke up with the tent walls partially collapsed. Two feet of snow had fallen overnight and buried both my camp and that of the Japanese team. The snow stopped piling up right below the tent's vents. If it had kept on snowing and I hadn't woken up, I would have suffocated. The Hilleberg tent is highly waterproof, so sealing the vents would make the tent airtight. This was my first expedition in years where I had had to contend with heavy snowfall.

After eating and cleaning up, I stepped outside of the tent to see what the world looked like. The clouds were heavy and low hanging, obscuring most of the landscape. A light breeze rippled the side of the tent. It was enough to create motion but little flapping noise. The air smelled cool and crisp. Every so often I caught a whiff of food from the Japanese team's breakfast.

The trail was completely buried in both directions; meaning travel would be slow and difficult. I spoke with Nori and his wife, the Japanese team, about the situation. We all agreed that it would be good to wait until a few big teams came through to pack the trail down. I was by myself and they were only two climbers. I thought it would be good to join forces.

"Nori, if it gets too late in the day, would you like to rope together for safety while we climb to fourteen thousand camp?"

"Yes, that is a good idea. Let me ask my wife about it."

"Okay, sounds good. I'm willing to wait a few hours rather than dragging a sled through deep snow."

"Yes, we are too."

I returned to my tent to let them have time to themselves. Nori's wife seemed to keep to herself and he did all the talking for them. From their perspective, adding an unknown climber was risky. I wouldn't have blamed them if they passed on adding a third person to their rope.

As building-sized crevasses abounded in the area, I didn't wander about. I spent most of the time in the tent, staring at my red home. The wind rippled the nylon, making a gentle fluttering sound. It was just strong enough to prevent the inside from growing too hot in the incessant sunlight.

Every so often, I poked my head out to see if anyone had walked by. No luck. The Japanese were doing the same, hoping that someone else would do the grunt trail work. As a team, breaking trail can be shared by all climbers, but by oneself, the work is grueling. Also, it's dangerous to walk unroped in a known crevasse field. I didn't want to make myself the sacrificial lamb by punching through a snow bridge.

By 2:00 p.m., I started to think I would have to march toward 14k camp alone. I began packing my gear, anticipating that I would have to be the trail slave. The Japanese packed their camp after arriving at the same conclusion. Just as I collapsed my tent to store it away, however, three climbers came into view around Windy Corner.

"Hey, Nori, looks like we're going to have someone help us out here!"

Nori looked at me then down the trail. He smiled, waved, and dove back into his tent. Unintelligible Japanese floated by on the light breeze. Though I didn't know what they said, the tone of their voices suggested excitement and haste. They wanted to ascend to 14k camp, too.

The three climbers walked by, heads down. They'd obviously been grinding for some time, being the first to march in the snow. The leader looked up at me, nodded, and put his head back down. He was focused on guiding his team through the terrain. The other two climbers didn't acknowledge me at all. It looked as if they had had a tough climb from

11k camp. From their dour expression, I wondered if they'd been caught at Windy Corner and were glad to be finally making their way out and around. None of them looked to be in the mood to chat, so I let them by without comment.

I was soon packed and on my way. Even though I was following in footsteps, the snow was still deep and difficult to walk through. I did my best to march in their footprints, half successfully. For a while, I felt like I was cheating at being a soloist.

"I should be out here breaking trails and taking my own path," I murmured to myself in the cool, unmoving air.

As the last words came out of my mouth, I glanced to my right. Only ten feet off the path was a crevasse. The edges were sharp and the bottom was invisible in the blue-black hole. The new snowfall partially obscured the edges. After examining the fissure in the ice, I walked back and looked at the approach. The edge was completely invisible. Had I taken my own route, I would likely have walked straight into an icy tomb. So much for walking by myself. Skis would have bridged the three-foot wide gap though snowshoes wouldn't have saved me. The only value of the crampons I wore in this kind of hazard was to help me crawl my way back out.

Reaching the bottom of the long climb to 14k camp, I paused to eat five shortbread cookies. I needed energy. The sun peeked through the clouds and began to cook me. Stripping off my parka, I continued the march up to the camp. It took twenty minutes to ascend the hill in strong winds. The altitude, sun, and wind made the walk feel like an hour. Snow blasted off the 16k ridge.

Once I crested the top, camp 14k revealed itself in all its jumbled glory. Lumps of snow protected the tents and there were little encampments everywhere. Cooking teepee tarps dotted the landscape. After seven days of trekking up the mountain, I had finally reached my home away from home.

It was 4:00 p.m. The wind was light on the flat glacier that fanned out into a plateau. After spending days at 11k camp where the safe camping area was compact, 14k camp felt like it had infinite space to spread out. Tents were not stacked on top of each other. Rather, there were walking paths between the tent walls.

Yet, there were still dangers to consider. I couldn't camp too close to the headwall that led up to 16k, as the face had avalanched before. As I looked out toward the Edge of the World, I saw the familiar orange human waste crevasse marker sticking up out of the snow at a distance from the camp. From this far away, the crevasse it marked was invisible. It was my reminder that though the area looked safe and friendly there were hidden dangers lurking just below. The absurdly large crevasses I had passed while climbing the thousand-foot high hill to reach here reminded me that this glacier moved. There were more dangers lurking beneath the soft shell of snow.

I knew I had plenty of daylight so I spent some time selecting an ideal campsite. Several spots looked promising but after probing them with my trekking poles I found hidden holes or hard ice. Eventually, I settled on a spot right along the main walking path through the camp. The traffic would be higher and that would give me the chance to chat with other climbers and glean information about conditions higher on the mountain.

While building my camp, I caught snippets of conversations about how the climbing was today. People seemed unhappy about how things were going high up. Absorbed with chiseling out a flat area, I promised myself to ask tomorrow what everyone was so grumpy about. The faint sounds of roaring stoves all around me filled the air, along with the aroma of ramen noodles flavored with beef, chicken, pork, or shrimp.

Each of these smells was unique and reminded me of my college days. As gentle breezes swirled around the camp, the different aromas created a strange, heady zoo of fragrances.

After living on a slope for the whole time at 11k camp, I was mindful of how level my tent site was. I took an extra hour scraping and testing the ice. I knew I would have to live in this camp for several days and I wanted it to be as comfortable as possible. The extra effort paid off when I pitched my tent. Setting the stakes and guy lines was easy. In ten minutes, my red tent was up and I was home.

Walking around my camp, I chopped blocks of snow out and built a windbreak. Many tents around me were nearly invisible below their four to five-foot snow walls. People seemed to have put significant effort into protecting their tents from the wind. It was a good policy—spend time on your camp now and live in relative comfort later. Although I moved slowly because of the altitude, I felt surprisingly good. No headaches or upset stomach bothered me.

On the headwall, I watched climbers descending from higher on the mountain all evening. I could see a tell-tale streamer of snow flying far off the top of the ascent. It was evidently windy up there. One climbing team walked close by after they had descended, each of them fully geared up, so I couldn't tell what they looked like. I asked the last unroped climber how it was.

"Windy. Really bad winds. We placed our cache at 16.2k but expect it'll be blown all over the place," he said.

"Why's that?" I asked.

"The surface was hard wind-blown ice. We used our steel spade but it barely made a dent in the surface."

"How far down did you bury your supplies?"

"We were lucky to get them under one foot of ice blocks. Even though we stomped them down, I doubt they'll be there when we go up."

"Sounds pretty rough."

"This is the last comfortable camp. Above here life becomes crappy."

"Thanks for the warning. Have a good evening."

The anonymous climber bade me good night and trudged away, catching up with his partners. As he walked off, thoughts of being trapped at 17k camp filled my mind. Every description I had been given about being high on Denali was uninviting.

During the night, I heard a dull, low roaring. As there was still plenty of light, I decided to see what was causing it. After wriggling around in my sleeping bag to get into position, I poked my head out of the tent and scanned my surroundings. Nothing seemed to be going on in 14k camp itself and there was little wind. But when I peered up the headwall, I was shocked to see a massive cloud of snow blowing off the top. The wind was tearing at the crest far above. Although the top was three-quarters of a mile away, the roar of the wind sounded like a distant waterfall.

As I lay down and worked on falling asleep, I couldn't get rid of that image of the massive snow line blowing off the top. Thoughts of the storm the characters in *Minus 148°* dealt with filtered through my mind. What I had heard and seen kept my mind spinning for an hour until I finally fell back asleep.

~

Reaching a new plateau is both exhilarating and exhausting. Once you are there, your new challenge may seem insurmountable. Don't lose heart. Remember how the first challenge looked and how you overcame it.

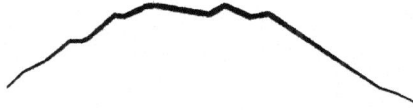

Chapter 12
May 18, 2016
Rest day at 14k camp

After nearly a week of struggling up the mountain, I enjoyed my first night at 14k camp. The best part of it was that I felt in excellent shape when I woke up, in contrast to how I felt after the first night at 11k camp. I had worried that I would wake up with a raging headache, but the altitude hadn't bothered me at all this time. Staying at 13.5k camp had paid off, and after ten hours of sleep, I was the only person out of his tent at 5:00 a.m.

I had nothing planned other than milling around camp acquainting myself with other climbers. The lower part of the mountain presented no particular technical challenges. As I looked 1,000 feet above me, to the top of the headwall, I knew that there were fixed lines up there, though they were invisible from this distance. They made travel up this massive half-mile high wall of ice and snow relatively safe for teams moving up and down the mountain.

Apparently there were two sets of fixed lines running near each other. The right line was dedicated to upward travel and the other was used for downward travel. The steepest part of the slope was around 50°. That's not steep by mountaineering standards, but should one fall unroped there was a good chance of serious injury or death.

Later in the morning, people started appearing and wandering around camp. My closest neighbors, two American men, nodded at me when I caught their glance. Trevor and Nick ended up being excellent neighbors. They were approachable and humble as well as athletic and strong, at least as far as I could tell under their down parkas.

Climbing the headwall to high camp.

"Hi guys, how are you doing?" I asked.

"Well, thank you. Checking out the fixed lines?" Trevor asked.

"I can't see them from here, but I assume they're in good shape," I replied.

"Yes, they're pretty good. Though the first thirty feet of the up line are buried under ice right now," said Trevor.

"That must make climbing tough."

"You bet. Yesterday it was a total shit show," said Nick.

"How is that?"

"People climbing down were yelling at the people using their descent rope to ascend," said Nick.

"How do people deal with that, anyway?"

"Not so well yesterday. What we did the day before is use the down rope to climb up, then we swung over to the up rope and swapped over," said Trevor.

"So you avoided being the troublemakers?"

"Something like that. I hear the park service is going up to replace the lower section of the fixed line," said Nick.

"Oh? I thought the guiding services maintained the lines?"

"That's what we thought, too. But Steve, the ranger we met, said that they're unofficially maintaining them now. Maybe they got sick of hack jobs," said Nick.

"That does make sense. If they have to deal with all the wreckage, maybe it's better. Perhaps that's included in the increased permit cost," I ventured.

"Maybe," said Trevor. "That thing is nearly double what it was just a few years ago, according to what I've seen online."

"Even though the permit is higher, this still has to be the cheapest of the seven summits to climb," I pointed out.

"You thinking of doing all of them?" asked Nick.

"We'll see. I want to see how well I do on this first," I replied.

We chatted some more about the weather, climbing conditions, and crevasses. It was enjoyable to find some independent climbers. They gave me insight into how the camp worked, where things were, and how people dealt with living on the mountain.

Later in the morning, three climbers made their way up the headwall. No one else seemed to be following. A few other climbers walked by and I asked about their experience higher up. They said the surface was rock-hard. They had buried their cache right at the top of the ridge at 16k. But they explained that "buried" is a relative term.

"We expect that when we get up there next, all of our stuff will be blown around," one climber said.

"You couldn't chisel in with your steel spade?" I asked.

"Nope, not at all. We're lucky to have put some ice on our cache. We needed pick axes," another said.

I had read the surface higher up was hardened. Little did I imagine that it was impenetrable. I was sure there must be areas that weren't as hard as rock, however. For all the stories I'd heard of teams building snow caves, there had to be some soft snow. Plus, people at 17k camp had managed to build snow walls.

I concluded that this team had been forced to dump their supplies and descend before completing the job. Maybe the strong winds of the last few days had threatened to blow them off the mountain. They seemed somewhat demoralized, so I didn't press them for further details.

In the afternoon, a young climber with wild curly hair and a scraggly beard walked over to my camp and struck up a conversation. He had a pleasant Australian accent, which made the conversation more interesting. Some words he used were alien to me, just as I'm sure my American dialect sometimes must have confused him.

Felix and his team had been on the mountain for some time. He said his climbing partners were up at high camp. I asked why he wasn't with them.

"When we tried to move to high camp, I developed a horrible headache up there. The altitude got me immediately," he said.

"Probably a good choice to come back down. You have an extra tent?" I asked.

"Yes, it's the yellow one over there."

I looked where he pointed and was somewhat surprised that it wasn't protected by any snow wall.

"Have you ridden that tent through a good windstorm yet?" I asked.

"No," he said. He paused for a moment. "Do you think I need to build a wall?"

"If you're feeling up to it, I would. I know my tent can handle Antarctica, so I only bothered to build a half-wall. I use earplugs for the rest."

"You were in Antarctica?" he gasped.

"Sure was. Set the record for the longest solo expedition to the South Pole," I said.

"What happened?"

"All sorts of things broke and I became sick down there. It was a rough start."

"Sounds like you made it through, though."

"It was the best time ever. Every day was a butt-kicker. There were so many days I had to build a massive wall to deflect the wind."

"So you know how bad it can get?"

"On bad days I couldn't see farther than a few feet," I said with a laugh.

"Oh, my gosh. Were you scared?"

"Sometimes, sure. But I was too occupied with moving forward and surviving to worry much. I knew what I had to do every day. How about you? What do you do?"

"This is my first big mountain. I do a lot of solo canyoneering," he said, smiling.

"Are you crazy? I thought I was nuts," I replied in shock. Among the things I learned in Utah was that canyoneering solo was extremely dangerous. One might end up like Aron Ralston, cutting a hand off.

"No, not really. I know all the canyons I travel. And they're different than those in the states," Felix said.

"You're braver than I am. Getting stuck in a canyon alone and having to hack my arm off isn't how I want to go."

"So you've seen that story? I don't do that sort of stuff. It's calmer in Australia."

"Except for all your lethal snakes and bugs," I chided.

"Well, there are those. But they're not too bad if you know what to watch for."

"How about if I visit? You could be my tour guide and keep me out of danger."

"Sounds good to me."

I talked to him some more about his climbing partners up high. I discovered that one of them was Tony, the skier I'd met near Squirrel Point during the windstorm.

"Tony did say he met a crazy solo climber out there. Guess that's you!" Felix said.

"Sure enough. It's not like we spread out here. One way up. One way down," I replied.

"Pretty much. At least down here. Did you think about doing some of the other routes?"

"I did and put them out of my mind. I figured I had better survive the West Buttress first. If I have a good time with it, then I'll come back."

"Probably a good choice," he agreed.

We moved on to other subjects, including what each other's countries were like. I love the opportunity climbing provides to chat with people from all around the world. Denali draws a serious international crowd, and Camp 14k was a one-stop-shop for meeting foreigners from virtually every country on earth.

The rest of the day passed uneventfully. I ended up sitting around much more than I should have, as I was fatigued. I didn't feel particularly bad, but I had little energy. Maybe it was the single hauling up the mountain. I began to question my tactic. Even though I didn't want to climb up and down, maybe it was too much.

Once the sun dipped below the far mountain peaks, the temperature plummeted and everyone donned their heavy parkas. The snow, reflecting the sky, turned blue. The sound of MSR white gas stoves filled the air, along with the scent of ramen.

At 8:00 p.m., the entire camp fell silent as everyone turned up their radios to listen to the weather forecast. There were so many speakers playing the same broadcast that I didn't even need to turn mine on, but having it powered up and listening on my own made me feel more confident.

Several guides had professional, programmable radios. I only had my chunky yellow Motorola FRS unit. It was better than nothing, but after chatting with a guide I found out the professional unit had a better antenna. It picked up broadcasts at 11k camp that were inaudible to me.

The forecast was for high winds aloft during the week. That put doubt in my mind that I would be able to climb higher in the next few days. I tried not to think about the roar of the wind above me, but it was difficult to ignore the sound of it as I fell asleep.

~

Take time to recuperate and regroup for the challenge ahead. Take holidays and make new friends. You never know how you might help them and how they can help you.

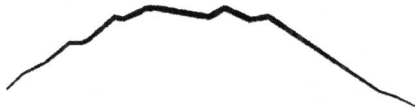

CHAPTER 13

May 19, 2016
The High Day

The morning was calm with light winds. Scattered clouds danced across the sky. The strong wind from last night had abated, though when I looked outside the tent at 6:00 a.m. there were no other climbers out yet.

I started wondering if Denali was more of a late start mountain. It might be that only when teams set off for the summit did they leave early in the morning. At this time of the year there was never real darkness. While the sun idled below the ridge, the air was crisp and cold, hovering at 0ºF. After Antarctica, these temperatures were comfortable.

As I felt pretty good, I wanted to see how far I could climb up the headwall. The West Buttress book suggested acclimating at 14k camp for at least four days before moving up the mountain. That seemed like a long time at camp, though I knew that if I moved too high too quickly I risked developing lethal high-altitude cerebral edema (HACE) or high-altitude pulmonary edema (HAPE).

I had fared well on Orizaba two years previously, and that mountain was 18,300 feet. I remembered the stories of other climbers. Sometimes you might have twenty problem-free climbs above 20,000 feet and yet develop severe altitude illness on the twenty-first. There was no way to predict what would happen.

The only way to find out how well I would do was to try it. If I had been in my twenties, I might have considered one crazy run to see if I could make it to 17k camp, but I didn't want to push my luck. My goal for the day was to reach the top of the 16.2k ridge and then turn back.

Only if I felt well at that point would I consider moving forward to see what 17k camp was like.

I wanted to get moving, so I made breakfast and forced it down. As expected, it was more difficult to eat at this altitude. I knew that as I moved up the mountain my appetite would deteriorate and that I would face a constant fight to feed myself. Even though I needed more energy the higher I went, the desire to eat would get weaker and weaker.

Climbing at high altitude is an exercise in mental discipline. Most of the time I hold it together. Sometimes, nonetheless, my emotions overwhelm my logic. I had already let the heat at 11k camp discourage me a few days before, but as long as I kept such incidents to a minimum I should be okay. Without a team, I had to be my own cheerleader.

After I had finished breakfast and sat on the cold plastic can masquerading as a toilet, I packed for the climb. I loaded a full day's rations and three liters of water in my pack, along with sunscreen, additional sunglasses, and my first aid kit.

My boots felt comfortable so my feet hadn't swollen at all overnight. So far my body had adapted well to altitude. It took some effort to snap on my crampons, though, as they were barely big enough to fit on my size 12 Millet Everest boots. I had to be cautious with them as I hadn't brought an extra set of crampon extension bars. Looking at the rocks higher up, I now realized this was a mistake. The two things I couldn't live without above 14k camp were crampons and an ice axe. If either failed me, I would be stuck. I would be forced to ask for help from other teams, endangering them.

Sighing, I shook my head as I realized how dumb it had been to skip bringing a spare set of crampon extensions. The cold combined with the rocks and a stumble might easily break one. Granted, thousands of climbers never had such a problem, but the stories others told me of flopping crampons were enough to make me swear to bring a spare set of bars in the future. At least I had a spare ice axe with me.

Other teams had already begun to make their way up the mountain by the time I left. Walking up to the headwall was both exciting and intimidating. This was by far the steepest part of the climb. The upper portion had the fixed lines that all teams relied upon. I hoped to reach them and then make my way to the ridge.

One team of twelve climbers had stopped halfway to the fixed lines. Under the instructions of three guides, they began placing snow pickets and lined up to do some practice ascents. The lead guide was an Asian female. Although she was short, she could sidestep up the steep slope faster than I could walk up the stairs at home. I instantly appreciated how much she must train in the off-season to be a guide. Or perhaps she just came from the Himalayas?

Step after methodical step, I approached the fixed lines. The footprints in the snow made travel relatively easy. I used the rest step as I moved up. This helped prevent me from overexerting myself. Though progress seemed slow, I made my way steadily up the hill. Without any trees around me, I felt very exposed—not that they would be of any help. Should I start sliding, there was nothing to stop me. By the time I reached a relatively level spot below the fixed lines, I was at 15,000 feet and decided to take a break.

The view was spectacular! 14k camp looked like a colorful ant farm a thousand feet below me. Clouds moved through the canyon beyond the Edge of the World. I was about to take my pack off for a rest when I recalled the story of another solo climber who did the same thing a few years before. He took his pack off for a rest but, in a moment of inattention, the pack slid away from him. His natural reaction was to leap for it, and in an instant both he and the pack were rocketing down the slope. In moments, he was dead. The ranger report read, "The victim had injuries incompatible with life." The penalty for error was absolute here.

Instead of taking my pack off and setting it down, I knelt and pounded out a seat. This allowed me to sit and enjoy the view without dismounting my pack. I had packed food and water into my parka so all I had to do was unzip it and drink. Sitting with my face to the view violated the climbing rule of always facing the danger—that is, looking uphill in case of an avalanche, rock fall, or climbers dropping gear. The hill here was so steep, however, there was no way to sit looking up, as I would just fall over backward. I had to take my chances.

After resting for fifteen minutes, I was chilled and needed to continue my way up. As I stood up, my stomach made the most unsettling grumbling noise. It lasted for five seconds. It wasn't the subtle, embarrassing type; rather, it felt like the rumbling that immediately precedes a massive spat of diarrhea. I froze.

Thirty seconds and then one minute passed. Nothing happened. My stomach was apparently stable once more.

"Great," I told myself. "Way up at fifteen thousand feet is the first time my stomach decides to go crazy."

I wasn't sure what to do. Should I return to camp in case something happened? Could I risk climbing higher? If my stomach became unsettled on the fixed lines, I would be in trouble. I sat back down for several minutes, waiting. My stomach made no more noise, yet it didn't feel perfect.

Placing my face in my hands, I sighed. I knew the right choice was to go down. So much of me wanted to enjoy the day and climb higher. My climber's ego told me to make the ridge, to go for it. The survivalist told me to drop down, to come back tomorrow.

"The mountain isn't going anywhere," I said aloud. "It only took me an hour to get here. Coming back will be easy enough."

Looking out, away from the headwall, I surveyed the scene. Distant puffy clouds floated beyond the Edge of the World. Little ants marched around 14k camp. The world was silent. Sunlight drenched the slopes. Though wind blew off the ridge higher up, the scene was a perfect daydream. I was truly blessed to enjoy this view near the top of North America.

Walking down and back to camp took half an hour. The snow turned slushy and I sunk to my knees. No other climbers ascended as I made my way to the tent.

Felix, who was camped nearby, walked over to talk.

"How did it go up there? Were the conditions good?" he asked.

"Sure were. It was all good until my stomach rumbled like something was wrong."

"Oh. Maybe it was a good thing you turned around. You don't want to be on the fixed lines if you need the toilet."

"That's what I thought, too. I didn't want to try and drop my drawers mid-ascent."

Felix laughed out loud. "That could be rough."

"How long have your climbing partners been at 17k feet?"

"Several days. I don't have any way to communicate with them, so I hope they're alright. The wind has been bad up high."

"Yes, I saw it yesterday and today. I was worried about topping the ridge and being blown off."

"It does happen. I came back down until I feel better."

I raised my eyebrows and nodded.

"You'll be better soon, I'm sure."

"I hope so. I probably just climbed too fast."

We continued chatting about climbing conditions, what we had done, and what our plans were. Felix was a congenial, unassuming guy. He had no ego and was completely personable.

Later that evening, as I ate freeze-dried beef stroganoff, clouds crawled over the mountain. They began zipping across camp, obscuring the headwall. The radio forecast warned of heavy snow and winds tonight.

After eating, I added another layer of snow blocks to my camp. Although my tent was solid, I didn't want to take any chances. Denali is a famously stormy mountain. Avoiding becoming a rescue casualty was a top priority for me.

As I lay down, snow began ticking on the tent. Wind ruffled the nylon, flowing around the snow walls. I pulled my shovel inside just in case.

Looking at 14k camp from 15,000 feet.

~

Enjoy the view from the top of your achievement, whatever it might be. Even if it's not where you planned to end up, you never know when you'll have another chance to savor the moment.

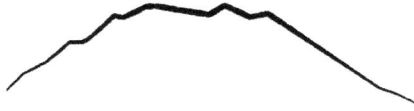

Chapter 14
May 20, 2016
Arctic Blizzard

At midnight I woke up and found myself in darkness. It was as though a dark cloud covered the sky. I guessed it might be snowing from how dim the light was, but I didn't hear the "prick-prick" sound of snowflakes striking the nylon shell. The air was nearly calm.

Looking at the tent walls, I saw they were bowed in, as though a bear slept against the outside.

"That's weird," I said to no one in particular.

The sound of my voice was muffled. I pulled on my light down jacket, unzipped the inner door, and was greeted with a pile of snow pouring in through the vent window.

"Whoa, I'm getting buried here!" I exclaimed.

I battered the outer shell door to knock off the snow. All at once the dusky Alaskan light poured in as through a single porthole. My tent had transformed into an igloo. After several more hand slaps, the thick shell of snow slid off the door. Drawing down the top zipper, more snow poured inside the tent from the roof.

Looking out, I saw there were two feet of snow piled up around the tent. My sled, ice axe, crampons, and CMC had vanished under it. Snow had piled up and half-covered the vent, meaning that if I had slept much longer both vents could have been sealed off, suffocating me.

"That would have been a heck of a way to go, silently slipping into a carbon dioxide coma," I mumbled as I donned snow gear over my long woolen underwear.

I stepped out in my boots into the thigh-deep snow and looked around. Other teams were already busy extricating their tents from the deluge. It was midnight and everyone was up. I grabbed my shovel and began scooping snow away from the tent, focusing on trenching my way around between the tent and the snow wall as that was where the most snow had built up in the few hours I had slept.

The snow was still coming down and as soon as I finished clearing one part of the trench another part of it began to refill. I had heard that three feet of snow could fall in a single night on Denali. Two feet had already fallen and the storm showed no signs of abating.

It took another half hour to free my tent from the crushing weight. As soon as I had made a full loop around the tent, I saw that I could easily make another circuit to do it all over again. All the while I had to be cautious about tearing the tent with the shovel. Though I wanted to work fast and get back to sleep, fear of damaging the tent slowed me down.

I stopped and debated. Based on how fast the clouds were dumping snow, I could be out here the entire night. That would leave me wasted in the morning. Instead, I decided to duck into the tent and set my alarm for 2:00 a.m. I had to sleep yet I needed to protect my shelter. It felt like performing watch on a ship.

As soon as I had disrobed and snuggled into my sleeping bag, I fell asleep. It only seemed to be five minutes before my alarm sounded. Again, the tent was remarkably dark inside. I knocked the snow off and looked out. Another eighteen inches of snow had fallen in the last ninety minutes.

I sighed. "This is going to be a long night."

I repeated the midnight process of trenching and shoveling out the tent. It took another half hour. Three inches of snow piled up while I was shoveling. Denali was giving me a real dose of weather. All the other teams were outside digging out their camps. Those with snow block walls struggled to move the snow outside. Though their ice blocks were excellent windbreaks, they made snow removal an exhausting chore.

"Some good, some bad," I muttered.

My wall was half the height of everyone else's, so it wasn't a perfect windbreak. But being less tall made shoveling easier as I didn't have to sling snow clear over my head. As I had never experienced this level of snowfall, I thought the trade was worth it. My Hilleberg tent was almost immune to the wind. The half-height wall made the wind flow over the tent, barely affecting it, so that was all I needed.

I repeated the shoveling process two more times during the night and into the morning. By the time the storm abated, three feet of new powder coated camp. I ate breakfast and stepped out of my tent early in the morning to enjoy the storm clouds rolling below and around 14k camp. No one else stirred for several hours. They were exhausted from the long night of snow shoveling.

By late morning, people were milling around. The camp had come back to life but not by much. Felix came over to chat about the snowfall. He was worried about his climbing partners at 17k camp. He'd not heard from them since he left with a raging headache.

"I'm going to climb up and see how they're doing," Felix said.

"That snow is going to make a tough climb," I warned. "I wonder about the avalanche potential near the fixed lines."

"I think it should be okay."

"Please be careful. That was a huge dump of snow. It'll take a while to stick and settle."

"I will. See you in a while, mate!"

Felix gathered his gear and post-holed his way up the headwall toward the fixed lines. As light snow continued to fall, I lost sight of him. I hoped he would be okay.

I retired inside of my tent and took a nap. The night of shoveling had worn me out, too. In the late afternoon, I awoke and went back outside. I noticed that everyone was looking up at the headwall. There were two climbers in high-altitude down suits, one green and the other orange, making their way down the face. I wondered what was happening.

One of the park rangers was waiting at the edge of camp to meet the pair as they completed their descent. Their conversation was inaudible over the breeze. Then they shuffled off with the ranger toward the National Park Service camp two hundred yards away from the main camping area.

A short while later Felix trotted up to me, excited and out of breath.

"Felix! How did the climb go? Did you see how your friends are?"

"No, I couldn't make it to them. The wind was too severe, so I turned around."

"I lost sight of you before the fixed lines."

"It was tough going, post-holing all the way up. Did you hear about the Romanians who just came in?"

"No, what happened? Why did the ranger come to meet them?"

"Their tent shredded and blew away at 17k camp. They had to sleep in their suits and bags."

"Are you kidding me? The wind up there was insane. I couldn't imagine sleeping out in it."

"The craziest thing is they made the summit," he said.

"Oh, wow! Did they have any frostbite?"

"It didn't look like much. Nothing that they can't recover from."

"I'm amazed. I'm glad they survived okay."

"They looked like a father and daughter team. She looked pretty young. I offered them water but they refused."

"Maybe someone else did. It was good of you."

Felix shrugged.

"Hopefully the park has a spare shelter for them," I continued. "I'm sure they're done with sleeping under the stars on Denali for a while."

We chatted some more about Felix's partners. He was worried what state they might be in. If the Romanians had lost their tent, I too wondered how his friends were faring. They'd been up there for at least two days before I arrived at 14k camp. Everyone says that you want to spend as little time at 17k camp as possible. Human bodies soon wear out that high.

***

Later in the day, Felix came over with a peculiar request.

"I'm sorry to ask you this, but can I borrow your poop can? My teammates have our only one up high."

"They really didn't leave you with much down here, did they?"

"No, I've not gone at all since they left, so I'm feeling full."

"By this time, I'm sure you are. Well, I never thought to have to share it, but go ahead."

"Thanks a lot, mate. I'll go and drop the bag in the crevasse for you."

"I appreciate that," I said, patting him on the shoulder.

It felt strange to share the can, but on a mountain like Denali there isn't much room for modesty.

In any case, I had other things to concentrate upon. My fingers were cracked and bleeding by this time. I hadn't been drinking five liters of water a day, nor had I been very diligent about keeping liner gloves on my hands at all times. As a consequence, half my fingers had stinging gashes. Every time I touched anything, it felt like someone was jamming a sewing needle into the tip of the finger. Though the pain was momentary, it was beginning to get me down.

However I had brought super glue for just such a problem. Sitting outside, I pried off the cap. A big glob of super glue shot out and plopped onto my new $500 climbing pants.

"Awesome," I said, along with some choice four-letter words.

Anger rose up in me, until I realized how fortunate I had been. It was better to have the glue hit my pants instead of an eye. It could have been much worse. I used a chunk of snow to mop up the mess.

I was cautious as I glued each split finger. Without acetone, I had no way to unglue my fingers if I got it wrong. At best, I could cut them apart. That would be a perilous task, even with a razor blade. So I took my time. As it was, climbing with glued fingers would be horrid.

While I patched myself together, my mind wandered back to the Romanians. I wondered what it would be like to be trapped outside in a sleeping bag at 17,000 feet, alone in the gloom with 80 mph winds swirling around me.

I didn't want to find out.

~

Moments of triumph are sometimes followed by tough storms. Choose to turn your face into the storm and keep shoveling. It will pass.

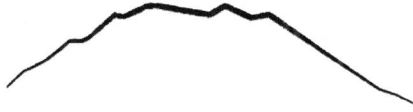

CHAPTER 15
May 21, 2016
Deep snow

The next day, the snow was still deep and hadn't yet packed down from the previous day's falls, but I wanted to attempt another climb on the headwall. I didn't want to be the first to post-hole my way up, however.

Felix came over and we chatted about climbing up higher together. We both agreed to wait until a roped team stomped out the trail for us. As neither of us had a rope, we didn't want to risk a fall. Another team said that no one climbed for days after a similar snowfall last year. No one wanted to risk being killed in a big avalanche.

My neighbors Trevor and Nick had been restless the previous day and were even more so this morning. They paced back and forth inside their tent and seemed to be going stir crazy from waiting for a weather window to climb to high camp.

The pair sported a Special Forces soldier look and wore black wraparound Oakley sunglasses. The way they stood and looked around was unlike any other climbers. Often the uniformed military personnel came over and chatted with them and it was clear there was a certain camaraderie that they all shared. It made making friends easy.

The best part was that they were all no-nonsense people. None of the uniformed military guys or gals had any air about them. They were up here on a training mission. Trevor and Nick were off-duty or retired, I wasn't sure which. This was a "just because" climb for them.

I asked how things were going with them.

"Every time I reach the fixed ropes, I get a raging headache," said Trevor. "I've tried several times and the result is the same. My climb is over."

"That's a shame. Have you been at this altitude before and had it happen?" I asked.

"I've only been this high before with oxygen or in an aircraft."

"Are you taking Diamox or anything else?"

"No, I didn't want to take that junk. I figure if I can't make it up the mountain without drugs, I shouldn't be doing it."

"You're a purist. Nothing wrong with that."

"If I relied on drugs and then I lost them, I'd be up a creek."

"Good point," I said. "Since I'm allergic to sulpha drugs, I can't take it anyway."

"So it's all or nothing with you, too."

"Yes. I have the same feeling. As a soloist, if I relied on tablets and lost them I'd be in a world of hurt."

"Why did you come solo up here? Windy Corner is pretty dangerous."

"I don't know anyone crazy enough to come climb this with me. Besides, I'm trying to string together a series of solo trips."

"I think it's a bit nuts," he said.

"Well, look at it this way. There's no one shooting at me or trying to kill me up here. What you military guys do is crazy."

"Well, it's a job, and the perks aren't all that bad," Nick chimed in.

"And I thank you for your service. I'd rather be alone in the middle of Antarctica than taking fire in Afghanistan any day," I confessed.

"That place is a pit," said Trevor.

"I travel a lot and it's on my 'probably never' list," I told them.

"Good choice," Trevor replied.

We all paused and looked around camp for a moment. Trevor and Nick glanced at each other, then back at me.

"We've been talking it over," said Nick. "The forecast shows bad winds for at least five days."

"So I've heard."

"Although we have food to stay longer, we won't have enough if we're stuck at the glacier for five days waiting for a flight," Nick went on.

"I've thought about that, too. Begging for food and starving at the runway doesn't sound fun," I said. The thought had been in my mind now for two days.

"Nick tried the climb yesterday but he didn't even reach high camp," Trevor said.

"The wind was too cold. I didn't want to freeze my nose and fingers off," Nick added.

"I don't blame you for turning around," I said.

"The forecast board was updated this morning. We're safe here but it's going to keep bombing up high for at least five days," said Trevor.

"Our summit window is pretty much closed," Nick admitted. "You never know what'll happen tomorrow."

"Good point. I have to leave myself a good margin, should anything go wrong. I don't want to end up in the news," I replied.

"The military team is taking off, too," said Trevor.

"They don't have enough supplies?" I asked.

"No, they are too close to their permit end date. With the weather forecast, their command told them to bail out," said Trevor.

"That's too bad. They've been real fun to have around camp," I said.

"Yah, too bad. Apparently, they've finished all their training goals, which didn't include the summit," Nick told me.

"But I bet that's the one goal they really care about," I ventured.

"Too true," said Nick.

"Well, guys, it's been a pleasure. The weather looks good right now," I said.

"It's probably good we're going. The forecast calls for rough times down here tomorrow," said Nick.

"Ah, great. It'll give me something to look forward to."

We chatted for a bit longer before I left them in peace to break camp. The military team was abuzz with activity, too. They were also breaking down their camp. It seemed like 14k would become a lot quieter by the afternoon.

***

After Trevor, Nick, and the military team had left, I walked over to Felix's camp. The sun was shining and heating up the glacial air.

"Hey, do you want to make a run up the headwall?" I asked.

"Sure. That sounds good. I'm tired of sitting around," he replied.

"There have been two teams up already, so there should be good footprints."

"Great. Get your gear and let's go for a walk."

I walked back to my tent, where I replaced my 40 Below booties with the clown-sized Millet Everest boots. After clicking in the crampons, grabbing my ice axe and water, I crunched back to Felix's tent.

"It's gotten really hot since noon," I observed.

"Yes, it has. It's not as bad as 11k camp, though."

"No kidding. That place sucked."

"That it did. Ready?"

"Let's do it," I said.

We started walking toward the base of the headwall. Although there was a trail, we still had to post-hole. Whoever walked ahead of us had a massive stride.

"Who are we following?" asked Felix. "These guys must be huge."

"No kidding. But I tried breaking a little trail to see if it was easier. It's even tougher."

"But barely?"

"Yes, barely."

By the time we reached the headwall slope, I had torn off my jacket, fleece, hat, and gloves. The breeze had quit and the sun was cooking us.

"I can't believe how hot it is," I said.

"I'm starting to sweat," Felix replied.

As we continued to make our way up the wall, I couldn't cool myself down. It felt like I had hot packs in my jacket. There was just no relief to be had.

After fifteen minutes of slogging up the hill, I started feeling nauseous.

"Dude, I'm sorry. This is way too hot for me," I said.

"You really don't handle the heat well, do you," Felix remarked.

"No, I guess not. After Antarctica, I like trekking in the real cold. The hot stuff kills me," I said.

"Okay, no worries, mate. I'll head up a-ways and see how I feel."

"Okay. Sorry. I don't want to abandon you up here, but I don't want to overheat and crash," I told him.

"You'll have to climb this in the early morning, Mr. Antarctica."

I laughed out loud. Felix was right—the heat bugged me way too much. We fist bumped and parted ways. He marched on up while I headed back to camp.

By the time I reached my tent, I was reeling from the heat. I didn't feel good at all. Though I'd stripped off everything I could, it felt like heat exhaustion. I tried to lie in the tent, but the temperature inside skyrocketed in the sunshine.

I opted to sit outside on the poop can. In a mere half an hour, I went from feeling warm to exhausted. After drinking a full liter of water, I still felt cooked. I stripped down to my underwear and partly pulled up my wool shirt. It felt like being in Death Valley in summer.

I tried to cool off by leaning against the snow block wall, but it took several hours before I felt better. While I recovered the camp came together for a pull-up contest.

A large crowd formed around a snow pit, which was spanned by a long-handled ice axe. Contestants cranked pull-ups while the audience counted out loud.

One of the guides told his people that he wasn't comfortable with them competing. He didn't want any of his clients to be injured and ruin their climb. It was good to hear a guide watching out for his team. Some people, it seemed, were taking needless risks. I overheard one guide talking about clients of his who were suffering avoidable frostbite after ascending in dangerous conditions.

Watching the fun the others were having helped take my mind off how bad I felt. As much as I wanted to join in, I still felt terrible. Everyone else was in their light down jackets, whereas I was only in my thinnest shirt and shell pants. It wasn't altitude or dehydration; I simply couldn't cool down and felt like vomiting.

After the sun finally dipped below the far peaks, the heat relented and I started feeling better. Felix came over in the evening to chat. He said he had been up the fixed lines, then turned around. The wind was too severe up high. I told him how I had overcooked myself and that I hadn't ever had it happen before.

"I'm glad you're okay. You didn't look good at all," said Felix.

"I don't know what it was," I said.

"Maybe you should've jumped in the snow to cool off."

"You're right. It would've felt a lot better."

"There have been a lot of teams bailing," Felix told me. "The bad weather has wiped out a lot of climbs."

"So I've seen. I'm starting to think I might have to bail out, too. Even though I've got nine days on my permit, the weather will be bad for at least five. And people have been getting hung at the glacier."

"Are you sure?" he asked.

"That's what I've heard, at least."

"I'd sure hate to see you go and then have the weather clear up."

"I know. I felt really bad all afternoon," I said.

"You didn't look too great when you turned around," said Felix.

"No, not at all."

In fact, I still didn't feel well. The possibility of passing out while going up the fixed lines had scared me. I'd never experienced that kind of overheating before, so I had no previous experience to compare it with. If it was hot outside, I adapted and did fine. But when it was cold and I overheated, I struggled. I realized I needed to change my training in the future.

"If you decide to leave, make sure you walk to the Edge of the World. Maybe it'll bring back the magic," Felix said.

"That'd be nice. Let me give you most of my supplies to make sure you reach the summit if you stay," I said.

"You don't have to do that. Are you sure?"

"Absolutely. You've been a great guy and I want to make sure you have a chance, especially since you're split from your team."

"Thank you. If you want it back in the morning, or want to stay, it's not a problem."

"That's fine. The other thing is, my permit expires soon, and I don't want to overstay my welcome."

"Oh, that can be a problem."

"I might be able to change it, though I'm not sure."

"I'm not sure how that works, but if you feel better it'd be worth asking," said Felix.

"We'll see in the morning. If the forecast keeps getting worse, it probably won't matter for me. No reason to stay ten days only to get skunked anyway," I said.

"That makes sense," said Felix.

We chatted for a few more minutes about Trevor, Nick, and the military team's departure. Felix said he had seen a lot of other teams packing up as he climbed down. There seemed to be a mass evacuation going on. Maybe they knew something I didn't.

As I ate dinner and fell asleep, I wondered what would happen tomorrow. If the wind remained as bad as it had been, climbing higher was just too dangerous. I hoped sleep would soothe my body and the conditions would mellow out tomorrow.

∾

If you go full tilt all the time, your body will give out. When you push your limit, you may go too far. Recover and find out what it will take to make it one step farther next time.

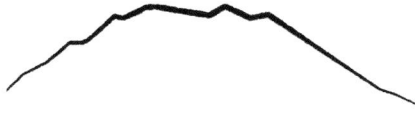

CHAPTER 16
May 22, 2016
Getting Out

Snapping awake at 5:30 a.m., I lay in my cocoon of down feathers for several minutes, sensing out how I felt. Was I nauseous? Did I have a wet cough? Was my head throbbing with a crushing headache? These are all signs of altitude sickness and each brings a host of potentially lethal problems.

I also listened for activity outside. No one stirred and no wind rippled the fabric of my tent. As I lay there, I analyzed my physical and emotional feelings. Was I doing better than yesterday after the broiling heat of the afternoon? Yes. I felt better. None of the overheated muscles had cramped up. My entire body had felt like it was on fire yesterday but now it was back to normal, or at least that was what I first thought.

Gingerly peeling off the eye mask, I opened my eyes to the black nylon darkness of my sleeping bag. Everything remained a blur. The drawstring of the sack of feathers was drawn tight, preventing cool drafts from coming in. By adjusting the position of my head and this face-sized hole, I was able to reduce the skylight pouring into my eyes. This was a trick I had learned in Antarctica. Instead of a wall of sunlight smashing into my face, I gingerly revealed myself to the new day.

There was no rush. Then again, no one ever seemed to be in a big hurry to start climbing in the morning on Denali. As I felt much better than last night, I started questioning my decision to leave. Doubt leapt into my mind. Sure, I had told Felix that I was bailing out and had given him seven days of food and fuel, but I also recalled what he had said in response.

"If you feel like staying, just come over and I'll give all this right back to you."

I could still ask for my supplies. There was no shame in that. Felix was clear he wasn't worried, as his cache high up contained enough food for him. To bail out as so many had yesterday held no shame.

Yet, I felt terrible about it. A vivid mental picture of my blue t-shirt from the Prostate Cancer Foundation popped into my mind. The bold white letters across it read: NEVER GIVE IN.

Was I doing just that? Sure, I had felt horrid the previous day. But that was a normal part of climbing high mountains. Or at least that was what I was told. When I was roped in with the military guys on Windy Corner, a few of them were dragged along. What one of the guys had said, as he looked about to vomit, echoed in my head.

"This is supposed to be fun, right?"

Military training instills impressive toughness. But that question was what I asked myself now. I knew Denali was a brutal mountain to climb, but was that made worthwhile by the fun I was supposed to be having? There was no one in the world to decide this for me. I had to decide it for myself. Here. Now.

I definitely felt better than yesterday—so much so that I thought maybe I was wrong to decide to leave. As waves of doubt and uncertainty coursed through my mind, a welcome sign of health greeted me. I was hungry.

Sighing once, and then twice, I rolled over and instantly felt famished. Glad for the distraction, I slithered my arm out of the sleeping bag porthole toward the cookies I had left in reach just for this purpose. Gingerly unwrapping them to prevent them from disintegrating into a crumbly, buttery mess, I packed one, two, three, four cookies into my mouth. Chewing and ramming them down as fast as possible, I worked to stave off the nausea of deep hunger. Feeling hungry always gave me a headache. The last thing I needed was a headache to fight. Previous doses of aspirin had done nothing for me, and there was nothing save emergency medication that would bring me relief.

On any other expedition, cold and hunger had been constant companions. Cold rarely bothered me, but the constant gnawing of hunger tended to get me down. Strangely I felt full after the cookies, though I was physically far from it. Four cookies was normally only a little something to keep me going during the day. My breakfasts were real power meals that would sustain me for three hours before I had to eat again. By the end of the second week on any other expedition, I ate or thought about eating constantly. Right now, I wasn't.

As soon as I had choked down the fourth cookie, my hunger completely abated. In fact, I felt quite stuffed. Slowly drinking from my small bottle to wash down the crumbs, I was astonished at how unnatural my rhythms of hunger felt. Normally, I clawed my way out of the sleeping bag to eat in the morning. Food dominated my thoughts as soon as my eyes popped open. Now, food was an afterthought.

"Come on, I must be hungry," I chided myself.

Two bites.

"Okay, now I'm not."

It felt like I was in a body that was not my own. I had morphed into a completely different person. My energy levels told me I was barely eating. I had read that a loss of appetite was normal on high-altitude expeditions. Others had warned me about it. I had failed to consider the psychological effect it would have on me, however. As far back as I could recall in my adult life, I had eaten incessantly. My active lifestyle and high metabolism had kept the food from turning to extra weight. Now, in just a few days, my body had become a complete stranger to me.

Humans need more calories when it's cold to sustain a 98.6-degree core temperature. In Antarctica, I consumed nearly 6,000 calories per day yet lost thirty pounds. The combination of dragging hundreds of pounds plus the extreme cold of Antarctica burned more than 8,000 calories per day. It was the ultimate weight loss program.

Denali was a different environment altogether. It assails climbers with sub-zero temperatures at night. In the day, air temperatures can rise well past 80°F. Temperatures in the tent exceed 100°F. The solar ovens of Denali's glaciers meant climbers need to endure large thermometer swings. My experience of intense hunger when it was cold was easy to deal with. I couldn't stop thinking about food. My solution was simple—eat more. But heat wiped out my appetite. Since most of my waking hours were spent feeling hot, much of the time I wasn't hungry.

Heat is relative on a mountain. Anything above freezing is quite warm for me. And since I wasn't hungry, I wasn't consuming enough calories to maintain my energy. Not only did I have to contend with altitude affecting appetite, but the heat also crushed any interest in food.

Not forcing myself to eat had caught up with me. It was easy to kick up the blood sugar by eating something, but I had let the heat and my lack of energy gnaw away at my spirit, my most valuable asset. Once I believed I felt bad and that reaching the summit wasn't impossible, I was finished.

If, indeed, I was deteriorating due to the altitude, I was a ticking time bomb. There was the chance that high-altitude illness would kill me. And then not only would my expedition be over, but my life, too. No summit was worth that.

A sudden gust of wind fluttered the wall of my tent. It was 8:00 a.m. and time to leave. I followed my ritual of scraping the frost off the ceiling and walls. The cup technique captured nearly all the frost. Looking in the dark, half-filled mug, I was reminded of the shaved ice cones they have in Hawaii. The frost had just the right texture, like it was ready to be doused in colorful flavored syrup. A vision of balmy winds shifting beach sand flitted through my mind. I realized I was disconnected from myself and needed to focus on the moment. Spending days staring at red nylon encouraged mental wandering.

My usual breakfast of cold cereal, whole powdered milk, and sugar took some time to eat. I spent the time contemplating whether I had made the right decision. Nothing was forcing me to leave. Sticking it out would be easy enough. To confirm my decision, I pried my head through the door and looked up at the headwall. There were small tails of snow flicking off the entire ridge leading to High Camp. A few cloud wisps clawed their way over The Edge of the World. The weather was destabilizing. Soon, a storm would descend upon 14k camp.

Forcing myself to shovel down the last spoonfuls of breakfast, I collected myself. I recalled Felix's recommendation to visit the Edge of the World to bring the magic back. I told myself to be positive about his suggestion. If there was a mystical place that would make me change my mind, it was the vertical-mile view to the Kahiltna glacier. A small glimmer of hope warmed my heart. What if, somehow, walking out to the viewpoint made me feel better? If it did, it would certainly be worth the walk.

Dear reader, a walk of a quarter mile may sound trivial. And normally it would be, for any mountain climber. But a solo walk with crampons through a crevasse field in deep snow is treacherous. There is always the risk of falling into a hidden crevasse. Without snowshoes to distribute weight, the risk is far greater, not least because I wouldn't be towing a sled that might arrest my fall. Soft snow makes walking more like controlled stumbling. One wrong swing of my foot could punch the inch-long crampon teeth through my leg, making tough conditions infinitely worse. A short walk in the mountains can become an evacuation in an instant. With the recent earthquake, it was also possible that the cornice at the edge was weakened. It might break away, giving me my first, and final, mile-long free-fall. But it would be an attempt to bring back the magic, to build a positive attitude and create hope for a physical recovery. So, for me this 400-yard walk was utterly necessary.

Ramming down the remainder of my cereal, I looked at my pile of gear. The weather was deteriorating. Clouds rolled over the cliff above. They still looked friendly and fluffy, but menacing stacks of lenticular clouds had already enveloped Mt. Foraker. Denali would be worse when those high winds dropped down thousands of feet to our level. They would turn 14k camp into another blizzard.

Brush. Floss. Toilet. Clean.

"Maintain the body," I told myself.

Get going. Now. Shove feet into boots. Lace the boots. Pull on the jacket. Don the cap. Slip on the goggles. Glove the hands. Unzip the door. Step.

Leaping out of the tent, I snagged on the guy lines and fell to my knees. It was a good thing I didn't put my crampons on in the vestibule. Laughing out loud, I looked back at my tent. Nothing was torn or damaged except my already squashed ego. Good. I still needed this thing.

I plucked the crampons out of my protective snow wall, then flexed the straps and crunched off the built-up ice. Sitting on the poop can, I carefully pressed the cold steel onto my clown boots. The toes slipped in easily, but the heel tabs were a full half inch away from fitting. They had been snug, if difficult to put on, on previous mornings. What had happened?

Inspecting the crampons, I found chunks of ice buried inside the bars and preventing them from fully extending. Jamming the bar all the way back, I squashed the finger of my glove. It was a good thing I was wearing them or I'd have had a bloody hole in my hand. Everything in sub-zero weather requires speed but care. Work too slow and something freezes. Work too fast and injury waits. Always wearing gloves keeps the hands safe.

I yanked my glacier ice axe out of the block wall and rapped it against the crampons to clear the ice covering the handle instead of using my hands. I didn't want the ice to melt and refreeze on my gloves as I walked.

As I approached the ranger camp, I examined the latest weather update.

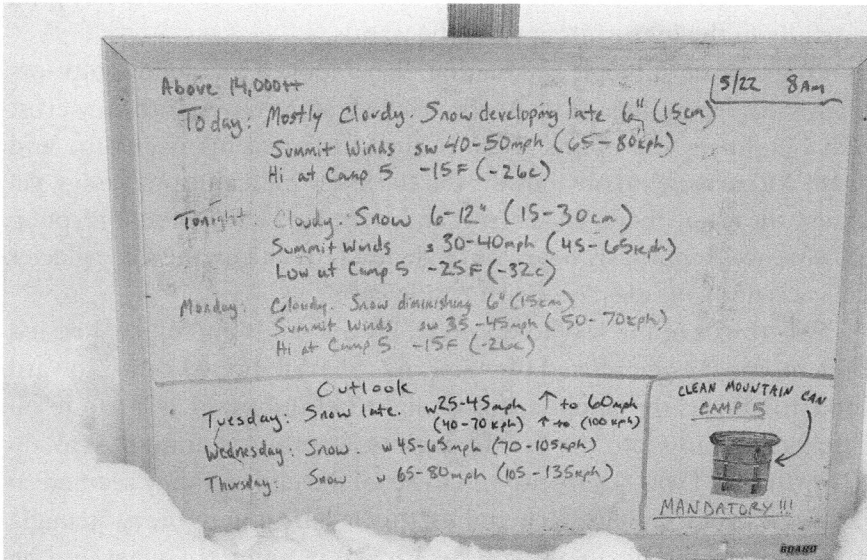

Weather board at 14k camp

My regret about leaving Denali vanished. It was going to be at least five days before the wind weakened enough for a summit attempt. Snow forecasts were often inaccurate but wind forecasts were always spot-on. Even if the estimates were off by 20 mph, it was still too dangerous to ascend. And the chance of the wind dropping from 80 mph to zero in one day was nearly zero itself.

Walking toward the open glacier, I was confronted by three pairs of crossed bamboo wands, which blocked the established trail toward the Edge of the World. Frowning, I cast about for an explanation. This set-up normally meant there were crevasses close at hand. I called out to two climbers walking on a nearby path.

"What's the story with the wands?"

"I think maybe it has something to do with possible crevasse danger."

"It seems funny to have three, but maybe it's an extra warning?"

"I don't know."

Thanking them, I took another look. The set of three pairs of wands perplexed me. Usually, one set of crossed wands was thought sufficient. No one was milling around in the ranger camp so there was no one official to ask. I took my chances. Bringing my ice axe into the ready position should I break through a snow bridge, I set out, stepping carefully in the footprints around the wands.

Progress was difficult and halting. What looked like solid footprints often sank me in knee-deep postholes. Soft snow covered the icy crust that caught my crampons. This, in turn, dumped me over time and again. There were no obvious dips in the snow indicating crevasses, yet I knew they were there. The narrow and seemingly bottomless NPS poop crevasse was ominously near. And I planned to walk on the same glacier. This was not your average quarter-mile stroll.

Two-thirds of the way to the edge, I found an island of ice. I rested for a moment and enjoyed the view. As the trail dipped down toward the cliff, 14k camp slipped out of sight behind me. I was alone on Denali. Stepping into the first footprints past the ice dome, I sank up to my thighs. I was so close to the rocks of the cliff, yet they seemed so far away. I told myself, "Remember, this is only a temporary struggle to get you to the next spot. You will make it, enjoy the view, and be stronger for it."

After post-holing for another ten minutes, I reached the slope that ended in the edge. I could not walk safely right up to the edge without being roped in—should the ice break away, I would fall a vertical mile and cease to exist. Instead, I lay on my belly and crawled my way to the rocks and peeked over. An upward blast of wind hit me in the face.

"Hello, void," I mouthed to myself.

The view made my palms sweat. Clouds floated by half a mile below me. The other side of the glacial canyon was miles away. The drama of the scene was stunning. Ice, snow, gray-black rock, and air were the only things I saw. Here was the magical view that Felix had told me to enjoy. He was right. It made me feel like I should continue.

Rolling onto my back, I saw what had hastened my decision to leave. Clouds now crept around the West Rib. Ribbons of snow flicked off the ridge thousands of feet above me. The morning was calm but strong weather approached. Spinning around on my stomach to go back down the slope, I played Superman, dragging myself down with ice axe and crampons. Once I was clear of danger, I stood up. A strong, cold breeze nudged me from behind.

"Better start moving," I told myself.

Past the ice island, my left hamstring violently cramped, dumping me on my side. There was absolutely no warning. My foot was pulled to my bum by an uncontrollable force and my throat tightened as I fell on untrammeled snow.

"Gah, oh geeze!" I howled.

Lying on my side, half buried in soft snow, I writhed in agony. I jammed my boot against the ice and tried to straighten my leg. The pain was intense. It was as though I had smashed the back of my leg with a hammer. It took a full minute to calm the muscle down enough to stand up again. The muscle twitched and rippled. Another breeze rolled around me. I needed to move faster, before a whiteout enveloped me, but I had to tread slowly to prevent another cramp.

As I walked up the slope revealing 14k camp, I saw a single ranger coming from the general camping area toward the NPS camp. It was strange as I hadn't seen any of them walking around that morning. He walked up to the crossed bamboo wands and stopped, staring at me. His posture was uninviting, as though he stared into the distance rather than at me.

One hundred feet away from him, I sank thigh deep into the snow as my right hamstring cramped again. This time, I twisted left, yelled, and unceremoniously fell onto my face in the snow. The goggles kept the snow out of my face, at least, but powder jammed up my nostrils. Shifting my body in the snow, I forced my right leg straight, and then pulled and massaged the uncooperative muscle while I snorted out snow. Struggling to right myself, I glanced at the dark green figure. He was emotionless and still.

Once I was back on my feet, I collected myself and I moved toward him and the crossed wands. When I was within earshot, the anonymous ranger finally spoke up.

"I put these wands here to prevent people from moving into the helicopter landing zone."

"Oh, crud, sorry!"

Odd, I thought to myself. How could a helicopter fly in this weather? I thought better of saying something smart, however.

"Don't worry, it won't happen again."

Nodding, the man moved off without saying anything more. He seemed irritated, as though I had broken some unspoken rule. This was the only path that people used to walk to the Edge of the World, but no matter—it would be pointless to debate the wisdom of being in an aircraft landing zone.

Back at my tent, I plopped down on my poop can to remove my crampons. Just as quickly, both hamstrings tightened, ready to cramp simultaneously. I shot up into the air, straightening both legs. I didn't want to embarrass myself any more than I already had, especially not in the middle of camp. Massaging both legs, I breathed calmly and drank the last gulps of water. I must have reduced my electrolyte level while climbing in the heat. I now endured the fruits of that mistake.

Unstrapping and kicking off my crampons, I dug my fists into the back of my legs and roughly massaged them into submission. Should my leg snap uncontrollably backward again, it might cause me to punch an inch-long steel spike through my leg. I didn't want to replace the mild nausea of yesterday with blood and searing pain. After several minutes of kneading my hamstrings, the twitching and tightness were gone.

Looking up the headwall, I saw a team of climbers near the fixed lines. I couldn't believe someone was climbing with high winds on the way. Seeing Felix loitering around his tent, I walked stiffly over to ask him if he knew who it was.

"That is the French team who camped next to me last night. They set off early this morning."

"Don't they know strong winds are on the way?"

"Yes, but they have a more advanced forecast."

"How so?" I asked, my curiosity aroused.

"They're paying for a professional weather forecast. There's supposed to be a clear, ten to twelve-hour window of no winds on the peak," said Felix.

"Sure hope they're right," I murmured.

"I think they just ran out of time. They seemed pressed and in a rush."

"And I thought I was crazy."

We both stood there for a few moments, looking at the French climbers as they disappeared over the lip at 16,000 feet. Long whips of snow were tailing off the ridge. The winds were above 30 mph already. I silently prayed that they would be safe.

"Are you sure you still want to leave?" Felix asked.

"Yes. I had terrible cramps this morning walking to the Edge of the World. I do feel better, but if the forecast is right, I'll run out of supplies before I can make it."

"I appreciate you giving me these rations. They'll come in handy, especially the chocolate."

"Don't worry about it. If it helps you make the summit, then it's worth it for me. Plus, I don't want to haul them down."

"When I leave, I'll be sure to give away as much as I can, too," Felix assured me.

"I appreciate your suggestion to walk to the Edge of the World. It was an awesome view."

"Sure thing. Of course. How close did you get?"

"Just enough to see over the rock, but no closer. The cornices farther down the cliff were huge."

"Without being roped in, I'm sure it was scary."

Laughing out loud, I related how I was busted by the ranger for going where I wasn't supposed to.

"You didn't hear?" asked Felix.

"No, hear what?"

"The ranger came round and told each team not to climb the headwall today."

"You're kidding! I thought they had a hands-off approach."

"Apparently it's supposed to be bad up there."

"Bad, yes, quite bad. The forecast showed 50 mph today, and then deteriorating through the week."

Felix's normally cheerful expression became serious.

"Wow! I really hope the French forecast is correct. Otherwise, they're in trouble. I'm really glad I came back down but I'm worried about my team. They've been up there a long time now."

"Your friends looked like solid climbers. I'm sure they've secured their tent and are waiting for their chance. Do you have a radio?"

"No."

"Whoa, it's tough to split up your team and leave them without communication." I tried to lighten the mood. "Too bad you can't send smoke signals."

Laughing, Felix seemed to rally. We went on to chat at length about climbing technique, what our original plans had been and how they had worked out. Felix admitted that he didn't know many things and hoped to pick up more skill as he went along.

"You're not doing too badly!" I told him.

"Thanks, it seems to be working out so far."

"I'll tell you, I learned things here, too. I didn't have everything perfect for my first big mountain solo. I certainly didn't anticipate the heat of the day on the glacier."

"You really don't handle the heat well. Maybe Antarctica changed you?"

"It must have. I grew up in San Diego, just south of Los Angeles. Perfect weather all the time."

"And you went from perfect to Antarctica and this?"

"Heck, yes. I love cold, terrible weather. It makes for a grand time."

"Maybe you are a little bit crazy."

"I have a very long line of people telling me that. It used to really bother me, as though they were making fun of me."

"I didn't mean that at all," said Felix, backpedaling.

"No, no, don't worry about it," I said, clapping him on his shoulder. "I now take it differently."

"How's that?"

"People can't imagine themselves going off and doing something so tough and uncomfortable. It scares them. My job as a motivational speaker is to tell them that yes, they can do something crazy. I don't recommend doing what I do exactly. I do tell them to embrace their own crazy, whatever it is."

"Like you said about canyoneering alone?"

"Absolutely," I agreed. "For all I've done, I would never explore canyons in Utah alone. I don't want to need to cut off a hand, like Aron Ralston."

"Canyons are different in Australia," he said.

"Good to hear. Let me know when you're in Jackson and we'll go climbing."

"Sure thing! Hey, would you like me to boil up some water while you're getting ready to leave?"

"Thank you, Felix. You're a thoughtful guy."

We chatted a while longer, then I excused myself to pack. Occasional puffs of breeze had brought in clouds that were darkening the sky. The sun was worked hard to beam through them, but the clouds were overwhelming its efforts. It was time to get moving. Standing outside my tent, I faced toward the headwall and looked up. There, far up on the hill, was my highest point, the flat area below the fixed lines. I pulled out my camera to film it as a record of what I'd achieved. Instead of being dour, I smiled.

Even though I wasn't going to reach the peak this time, I knew I'd pushed myself to the limit. I stumbled into 13k camp with the military, but my body had given out in yesterday's heat. There was no reason why it should leave any permanent damage. Denali would still be here. Remaining alive ensured another shot at the summit.

Looking over the piles of gear strewn about in my tent, I was tempted to be lazy, to ram everything onto the sled and barrel down the mountain. But I knew that overloading the sled was dangerous. If it overtook me and knocked me off my feet on Squirrel Hill or Windy Corner stopping would be impossible. I still had to be careful. As much as I didn't want to, loading the backpack with the heaviest items was safer. A lighter sled would be easier to control.

I packed slowly, savoring the thin air and enjoying the experience. There was no need to rush away with a sullen attitude, as I had seen others do when retreating without summiting. As disappointed as I was, I told myself to be happy with what I had accomplished. If sparks of dismay flickered in my mind I stamped them out before they burned too hot.

"No, you're doing the right thing," I told myself, speaking out loud. "If I developed HACE or HAPE as a result of overdoing it, I'd end up in a rescue situation. There's no excuse for being irresponsible. Bad weather will make helicopter rescue impossible and an emergency evacuation would be embarrassing. I can still bail under my own power."

Antarctica taught me to speak my thoughts out loud. Hearing my own words helps me think things out. Things that sound logical inside my head sometimes sound absurd when spoken out loud. Some would suggest that carrying on both sides of a conversation is the hallmark of a nutcase. I find it prevents me from doing something nutty instead.

As I finished packing the tent, Felix walked up with a pot of steaming water. Frost from the steam coated his dark, scraggly beard.

"Dude, you are awesome. I appreciate it."

"Of course. It's the least I can do," Felix said with a grin.

"It's actually a good thing you brought this over," I told him. "As I finished packing, I realized I'm a liter short of what I need. Perfect."

We performed a delicate two-person water transfer. Not a single drop of his courtesy was spilled on the snow.

"Last chance. You can still stay and see how things go."

I gave a short laugh. "It's tempting, Felix. Part of me wants to stay. But I don't have a real back-up, aside from leaning on your generosity."

"It's not a problem at all."

"Plus, you have two mates up high who might need everything you can bring."

"True. I'm glad I kept to my own pace. I wouldn't want to be up there in that wind right now."

"No kidding. I like bad weather, but being blown off a cliff—that's another matter."

Felix took a photo of me and promised to email it when he returned. Clipping on my crampons, hoisting the pack, and hooking up my sled, I gave him a last grin.

"You're a good man, Felix. I can't wait to see your summit photo!"

As I tied draglines to the sled, Felix asked what knot I used.

"It's called a taut line hitch. I learned it in Boy Scouts."

Untying the knot, I showed him how it was done. It was simple but powerful. With it, I could tension or slacken the line as needed, yet the knot didn't shift when weighted. It's not a climbing knot, but it comes in handy. Felix enjoyed the lesson and said he'd put it to use immediately on his gear.

Shaking hands, I bade Felix goodbye. A cold, strong breeze was now swirling snow around my abandoned campsite. It reminded me somehow of Hollywood Armageddon movies, where swirls of snow or dust always foretold problems. It felt like a cliché, except that I was living it. Looking back more than once, I waved to Felix and checked out the headwall in the same glance. It was a sweet moment, knowing I should make it out alive. A few people continued to mill about their tents, but no one seemed in a rush to do anything after the NPS warning.

Crunching along the heavily trafficked ice crust, I began my way down. Soon, I had dropped below the view of 14k camp and was on my own again. As I descended I kept an eye out for those building-sized crevasses, but they were barely visible because of the clouds that were now blocking the view. Strong wind gusts started shoving me around. Without the sled and hiking poles for balance, I would have fallen more than once.

As the slope became steeper, I lashed two 6mm cords under the belly of the sled. This helped slow it down so it didn't run me over. Though I had to pull at it sometimes, the two lines were a perfect balance of drag. Too much and I'd be working to go downhill; too little and it rammed into me, knocking me over.

By the time I reached 13.5k camp, walking in the path was difficult as it was obliterated by the drifting snow. If stronger winds rose and the clouds flattened the light completely, I would become lost again. I was headed for the crevasse zone on the uphill side of Windy Corner and knew that quite a few climbers had needed rescuing from holes around here since I came up.

Now, with the snow refilling the crevasses, there was a good chance they were bridged with deceptively weak snow. Add a whiteout to the mix and the danger increased. I had already nearly walked off the cliff and didn't want to repeat the experience. I pushed harder, extracting whatever speed I could out of my body.

After half an hour I managed to reach 13.5k camp. Little remained of the previous encampments. The military snow wall was fully buried and other caches were disappearing under the snow. Visibility had dropped to a hundred feet. The vast crevasse system, big enough to hide buildings, was utterly invisible. It was only a couple of hundred feet away from me, yet I saw nothing.

This felt like being in Antarctica. On so many days there was nothing to see—no landmarks, navigation points, shadows, nor anything else. It felt familiar and eerily safe. Although there was the danger of falling into an unseen crevasse, I had learned to accept traveling with my eyes open yet seeing nothing of the landscape. As clouds enveloped me, that same sense of calm learned three years before wrapped me in comfort. The wind gusted to 40 mph and was by now a raging storm. No matter. This was infinitely better than sitting in windless, sweltering heat.

I approached the crevasse system and had to make a choice. I could keep with the trekking poles to keep my balance—they'd saved me from plugging off the trail into waist-deep snow several times—or I could pull out my ice axe in case I slipped on the ice on Windy Corner. The trouble was that if I used the ice axe I wouldn't have the poles to counterbalance the unpredictable wind gusts. My ice axe would do nothing for balance during a badly timed blast of wind. It would only be useful for a fall or slide.

After a moment of debate, I reasoned that it'd be better to have the axe. Stumbling was annoying but trekking poles wouldn't stop a slide off the cliff. If I only partially punched through a snow bridge, I could stab the pick in and use the ice axe leash to hold my wrist. I would be stuck but still above the surface. Strapping the poles to my back, I loosened the axe and prepared for the worst.

Every few dozen steps, I crunched through hard snow and into soft. Sometimes I caught myself with the axe. Other times I stumbled a few feet from the track.

The trail vanished and then reappeared, over and over. In the white blankness, with driving snow at my back, I was in my element. Denali was giving me an epic send-off. She was making sure I wouldn't forget her. No matter what I did, how I prepared, or what I thought, she was in charge. That was fine with me. As powerful as we humans like to think we are, it only takes a modest storm to shut us down. How we respond to the storm is everything.

Then, far ahead, I saw two ghostly but colorful forms. One was large and dirty yellow, the other much smaller and turquoise. At first, I thought I was seeing things, but I hadn't been on the mountain long enough for that to happen. It took a month for my brain to begin playing tricks on me in Antarctica. These objects looked like nothing I had hallucinated before.

"What's that?" I asked myself out loud.

"I have no idea. I've not been out long enough to hallucinate. It has to be something man-made," came my reply.

At first, the forms flitted in and out of view in the flying snow. Then, as I drew within fifty yards, the two indistinct shapes turned into the unexpected—people.

"Who would be foolish enough to be out here, heading down in a storm?" I asked myself.

"Oh, that's right," I retorted. "Me!"

The wind ripped away my half-mad laugh. Another gust knocked me off my feet. While picking myself up, I tried to imagine who else would be out here. There was only one way to find out. I yanked my half-buried axe out of the snow and fought my way over to them.

The two figures seemed to be conferring with each other, not having moved for several minutes.

I yelled out a "Hello!" as I came closer.

The man looked at me, waved, and returned his attention to the much smaller person.

"Are you okay? Is there something wrong?" I asked. "This wind is becoming powerful enough to be dangerous."

"Yes, we are okay," the man answered in thickly accented English.

"Are you headed up or down? There are crevasses just ahead of here, and they're starting to fill in."

"We are headed down."

"Oh. Did you make the summit?"

"Yes, we did, and now we're heading off the mountain."

I paused. "Wait a minute, are you the two Romanians who made the summit and lost your tent at high camp?"

"Yes, yes, that is us. This is my daughter, Dor Geta, and I am Ovidiu Popescu."

"Great to meet you! Congratulations on your summit!" I yelled above the wind.

Even though we were only two feet apart, normal speech was impossible. I yanked off my hood so I could hear what the man was saying. Looking at his daughter, I saw fear in her wide eyes. It was unmistakable. They had survived losing a tent at high camp and somehow made it anyway. I guessed Dor Geta was just overloaded and wanted to be off the mountain.

"Would you like to rope together for safety? You could hold Dor Geta but there's no way she could hold you."

"We're not using a rope for this crossing, only a short line to stay close to each other."

I looked at their rope and saw it was a bungee cord. That revelation shocked me. I had seen they had a line when they returned to 14k camp, but it was beyond me that they were traveling without one across these crevasses and down the dangerously steep slope. It was tough enough travel in perfect conditions, but with this wind Dor Geta could easily be knocked over and slide off the cliff around the corner. Then I thought about how they had made the summit, even in terrible conditions. Who was I to question how they did things? What did I know? I hadn't made the summit.

"Okay," I shouted. "Well, if you two stay close to go around Windy Corner, I'll happily join you. That way if someone falls in, we can help each other. Plus, there are now two routes that I can show you."

"That is fine," Ovidiu shouted back. "We will lead, then."

Ovidiu spoke to his daughter for several minutes while she howled back at him, her expression a mixture of fear and frustration. Even though I understood none of the Romanian, I was blown away by Ovidiu's utter calmness. He wasn't yelling at her, pointing his finger, or anything. Considering the tough situation they were in, he was one of the calmest fathers I've ever seen. After some coaxing, he got Dor Geta moving again. I waited for them to draw ahead of me, then I followed.

For the first little bit, we did well. Our progress was halting, as Dor Geta had trouble discerning the trail. But when she looked around for a moment, she discovered the trail and kept moving. We carried on for several minutes until we came to the junction right before the crevasses. Dor Geta started heading down the slope, losing the trail.

"Wait!" I cried out.

They both stopped. I pulled up next to Ovidiu. "You can't go down there," I yelled. "You'll fall into a crevasse. See to the right?" I pointed up the hill.

He nodded, discerning the two trails.

"Someone created a second trail since you were here. The higher one goes over a different snow bridge and may be better."

Ovidiu called instructions out to Dor Geta and she turned up the hill for the higher snow bridge. At this point on Windy Corner, the slope steepened to the left. They had no trouble keeping their sled under control. They would be able to cross the upper bridge without losing their sled. I knew that the slope was too steep for me unroped, so I chose to keep on the lower path.

I watched them cross the bridge. It was eye-popping to see those two people going over that huge emptiness. If either took two steps to the left, they would fall into the void. And I would have no way to help if both fell in. Once they were across, I began stepping over the spider web of crevasses. Only days ago other climbers had fallen into them. Without a rope, I had no margin for error. As the wind was so strong, even if I yelled at Ovidiu, they wouldn't hear me. I would be gone.

Walking up to the first crevasse, I could barely see into the abyss. The wind whipped snow across the surface and into the void. I took a full step back and pulled the sled right up against me. If the traces yanked me back while taking the leap, I'd lose my balance and fall in.

I steeled my nerves. Breath in. Breath out. Breath in. Step, hop, and leap! I made it. Moving a few paces forward, I turned and pulled the sled across. It slid toward the crevasse but I guided it away and pulled it against me. One obstacle overcome.

Another twenty feet of walking brought me to a narrower crevasse. This one didn't demand a leap, only a giant step. The slope was steeper here, falling away to my left. At this point, should I stumble and start sliding, I knew there was a cliff waiting for me. Every step had to be perfect. I took absolute care with each foot placement. After fifty feet of walking, I came to the same crevasse the others had crossed, only lower on the slope. The snow bridge was wider here, but closer to the cliff. What a choice. Again, I stepped back two feet, pulled the sled up to me, and prepared to leap. The wind shoved me from the left and I lost my footing for a moment. This was turning into a real challenge.

Waiting for a lull between the gusts, I bided my time. The 20 mph wind was easy to jump in.

"If a 50 mph gust hits me as I make the leap…" I muttered out loud. "No, be quiet. Put that thought out of your head. Focus only on success. Otherwise, you'll make it happen."

This snow bridge was only two feet wide, but after the leap I would have to walk quickly to get away from the lip as a steep slope would pull me back toward the abyss. Should I pause, the whole thing could break, pulling me and the sled into the maw.

The wind slowed and I got ready to jump. Another gust caught me, nearly knocking me over.

"Have patience, Linsdau," I said. "This is no place to be careless."

Wait.

Wait.

The wind dropped to 20 mph.

Now!

"Gah!" I yelled as I leapt across the bridge, hop-stepping forward.

I had made it!

But after two steps I felt a powerful tug on my pack. I felt my eyes widen in panic. Leaning forward against the pull, I turned to look back. Oh no.

During the leap and hop I yanked at the sled. On the hard ice it had slid downhill toward the crevasse. The front was on the snow bridge, but the rear was in the air. It was slipping sideways now, half falling into the crevasse and yanking me backward after it. It looked like the *Titanic*, with only the bow visible above the surface. The rest of the sled, with all my gear, dangled over the chasm.

Instinctively, my hands shot to the rope. Gripping both the ice axe and line, I bent my knees and leaned back. Should I be pulled off my crampon-laden feet, I would be dragged head first into the crevasse. There would be no escape.

Flexing my back, I cried out in anguish and pulled with all my might. "Aaaargh!"

The sled slid sideways, farther toward the yawning hole. With another yank, however, it popped into the air, shot forward, and smashed against my shins.

"Whoa! That was close!"

Gulping the thin air, deep and fast, I collected myself. The forward edge of the sled had bruised my shin, but I didn't care. Ignoring the pain, I looked back at the crevasse. There it lay, uncaring and indifferent, snow blowing across it. The lifeless ice had no emotion. In my imagination, though, I envisioned a scaled, black claw retracting back into the blue-black void, waiting for the next climber to venture too close.

When I'd caught my breath I turned to see where the Romanians were. They had made their way along the high trail and were now descending. Though they were only fifty feet away, they were indistinct in the blowing snow. They hadn't seen anything that had transpired. My yells were ripped away in the wind. The way they were leaning into the building gale, Ovidiu was fully occupied with keeping his daughter safe. Getting her down the mountain was priority one. I was on my own.

Hurrying along, I caught up with them as Dor Geta stopped and curled up on the ground. She looked up at her father and yelled into the wind. He stooped over her and, above the roar, said a few comforting words. This guy was a bronze statue of calm. I walked up and asked how they were.

"We are doing fine. It is difficult for her," he hollered into my face.

I could barely hear him.

"I'll bet it is. We'll get around the corner and then we'll be safe."

Ovidiu coaxed his daughter into a standing position and pointed her down the trail. In a moment, they started moving forward. On this part of Windy Corner, there were two side-by-side trails, one above the other. Dor Geta took the higher trail while I stayed below them. As we rounded the corner, we could only see twenty feet ahead. The wind was shoving us along now. All the while, my sled slid, yanked, and did everything it could to pull me over the cliff a few feet away. Using my left arm, I pulled the traces and kept the sled as close to me as possible. My right arm held the ice axe at the ready. Should I slip, I would have only two seconds to stop myself before going over the edge. It was terrifying and exhilarating all at once.

The trail thinned and then disappeared. I knew this spot from being lost last week. My left hand screamed in fatigue. I had to rest. The line slid through my hand and the weight came onto my pack, pulling me around for a moment. The orange sled stood in stark relief against the matt gray air.

While I struggled with the sled, Dor Geta walked higher, Ovidiu following her. I turned to see them walking toward the cliff I had nearly walked off. Turning and almost leaping at them, I crunched on the rock-hard ice toward the girl, begging her to stop.

"No, you can't go that way!" I bellowed. "You'll die!"

Dor Geta looked back at her father, unsure what I was telling her. Her father looked questioningly at me.

"I made the same mistake last week," I explained. "If you keep going this way, you'll end up on a steep slope and the ice will break."

It was impossible to see the danger I talked about from where we were. Standing right next to Ovidiu, I put my hand on his shoulder and pointed with my ice axe.

"See—down there?"

Ovidiu squinted for a few moments. Then he saw it. A ragged wand with a black flag flailed in the gale winds. Turning to Dor Geta, he called out some unintelligible instructions. She responded, hopped off the upper trail, and began downward.

I patted Ovidiu's shoulder with relief and smiled. Returning the smile, he refocused and walked down the slope with his daughter. Waiting to make sure they were keeping to the path, I looked over my right shoulder. There, somewhere only a short distance away, was the ice face I had nearly walked off. Shaking my head, I turned and clomped down the ice slope to the pass.

When I caught up with them, Dor Geta was yelling at her father. I found out later she was just twelve years old. I had to admire her toughness. She reacted like any teenager would, but unlike the teens I knew back home she was capable of toughing out one harrowing experience after another.

Ovidiu carried on trying to soothe her, as much as he could in 60 mph gusts of wind.

"Are you two okay?" I asked.

"Yes, we are fine now. Thank you. You can go. We will be fine."

"Are you sure?"

"Yes, for certain. You can go."

Standing and looking at both for a moment, I realized it was time to take my leave. They had survived the crevasse field and avoided falling off the cliff. I didn't want to interrupt when Ovidiu was doing such a good job of calming his daughter. However he did it, I sure wish I could bottle it. It worked like magic.

"Dor Geta, keep your dad safe," I said. "You're doing great! I'll see you at 11k camp."

Nodding and smiling at me, the girl returned her attention to her father.

As I pulled away from them, I looked back. There they stood, on the cusp of the pass, wind raging around them, fully engrossed in conversation and paying me no heed at all. They had their own challenges to overcome.

Facing downhill, I was greeted with a very different scene to that which I had come through just five days before. Instead of packed snow, the surface was scoured any loose stuff. The few boulders that had barely peeked out before were now fully exposed. Rocks of all sizes were strewn about on the bare ice and when a strong blast of wind gusted across the saddle many of the smaller rocks skittered about.

All at once I realized what happens here during a windstorm. Regular snowfall packs the area in snow every few days. Then, when a storm blows up, all the loose snow is thrown into the air to fall off the cliff a half-mile away at Squirrel Point. As the wind intensifies, the small rocks that have fallen from the cliff face at Windy Corner are exposed and blown around. The transformation is dramatic. Winds have been clocked at 100 mph here. It is not a place to linger.

Tying a third line around the sled's belly, I began my descent. At first, the sled stayed behind me and under control. The hill wasn't steep, but the hard surface offered no traction for the sled. Even with three belly lines it slid sideways and past me, snagging on rocks and tumbling over.

All the way down the sled swung like a pendulum from left to right or flipped this way and that as it was caught by gusts of wind. The three 6mm cords had no snow to bite into and eventually balled up with ice, becoming useless. My crampons punched into the hard surface. I wasn't worried about slipping but I didn't want my gear smashed up. After several tries at having the sled follow me, I gave up and let it lead me down. This prevented the sled tumbling but it was very awkward. With multiple climbers, such a maneuver is simple. By myself, the extra downward pull made for a knee-crushing work-out.

More than once, I looked back toward the Romanians. They were barely visible on the pass. It was not until I reached the bottom that I saw them clearly again, Ovidiu still talking to his daughter. I imagined the comforting words he was giving her. I felt guilty, as though I'd abandoned my climbing partners. Though we weren't together, I felt as though I'd broken an unwritten rule. But I couldn't force them to come with me. They had to move at their own pace and they looked fine and relatively safe. If they could survive 17k without a tent, this hill and the next would be no problem.

Dear reader, I still feel guilty about walking away, even though Ovidiu had essentially asked me to. I debated putting this in the book. I couldn't force them to accept my company. Indeed, that might have only exacerbated the situation. They knew what they were doing. I felt bad for Dor Geta, nonetheless. I didn't like to leave them on their own, though I did offer some encouragement. If I violated some unwritten rule, I apologize.

When I reached the bottom of the hill, racing clouds swirled about the icy plateau, shrouding everything in formless white. The wind had increased to seventy miles per hour now. I should have felt extremely cold, yet I was completely warm. How was that possible? There was no sun, nothing to create warmth, yet here I was, jacket fully unzipped and flapping in the wind. Leaning back, I raised my head and laughed out loud, then let out several "Whoo-hoos!" The sound barely reached my ears before it was sucked away. It was simply spectacular. Horrid conditions were, I discovered, my favorite. I had come here to be blasted by Denali.

"Yes, bring it on! I love this!" I howled to the void.

The Romanians had disappeared in the blizzard. In fact, looking around, virtually everything was invisible. All I could see was the twenty feet of ice around me. Standing and staring for a minute, I saw no wands anywhere. They were likely smashed or blown away. I began examining the ground, looking for a path of crampon marks. There they were—indistinct, but still visible.

Following them, I gingerly made my way across the expanse, conscious of the huge drops close at hand. Should I wander too far to the left, a thousand-foot fall awaited me. I checked my GPS to ensure that I was walking in the correct direction. Though the GPS was helpful to find the chute at Squirrel Point, there was no track to follow. The path meandered a bit, avoiding crevasses and cliffs. I still needed to follow a safe route.

The ice became hard enough to prevent crampons from making discernible marks. Looking around, I found what I was hoping for. Not crampon marks, but pee stains. These marks of people passing by were again my salvation. Every twenty feet, I found another. Now, I had an immutable path to follow. They were the same marks I'd followed before, on May 14.

Although the ice was flat, the wind shoved my sled to the right and past me. It snagged on a chunk of ice and tumbled over. When the trace went taut, it yanked me around. I couldn't believe the wind could be so strong as to shove a seventy-pound sled around like that. I was thankful I had transferred my fuel to small one-liter bottles. Had I left it in the metal can, it would have cracked apart, spilling fuel everywhere.

I pulled the sled back to me, righted it, and set off again. This drama happened several times, twisting the tow traces. Each time the sled rolled past me in response to a gust of wind, showers of rocks and ice pelted my back and head. If I turned into the wind, I received a face full of marble-sized rocks. Each stung my cheeks and nose like a bee sting. I wondered how much worse it could get.

Travel was slow as I had to stop every dozen steps and find my way again. Without anything to navigate by, I walked cautiously. Through the haze of clouds, fog, and horizontally blowing snow, I trudged on. I thought about the father-and-daughter Alaskan team who had made camp at the base of the hill at Windy Corner. Had the wind been this strong then? Was it stronger? I wish I knew. Having a gauge of what level of weather caused people to hunker down would be comforting.

After a few more minutes, the clouds cleared and I saw the lip of Squirrel Point. Had I walked fifty feet to the right, I would have fallen off the high cliff. I was more than ready to get off the plateau. As I closed to within one hundred feet of the cliff, the wind picked up ferociously. I stopped and leaned back into it, holding my position. Rocks and chunks of ice struck my back, like someone poured a bucket of dirt on me from a ladder. Each impact stung. The noise from the clatter of rocks hitting my helmet was deafening.

The sled flew past me, running to the end of the trace and wrenching at my backpack, nearly spinning me around. Seizing the line with both hands, I took the weight off and leaned farther back. The sled started hopping up and down, fluttering like a kite in a hurricane. Then, to my utter amazement, it lifted three feet into the air, flipped upside down, and smashed down on the ice.

After what seemed like minutes, the wind finally let up and I fell backward, sitting down. My backward lean was so steep there was no choice but to land seat first. I desperately wished I were able to video the drama.

I couldn't believe how my sled flew, save that it was now laid upside down near the edge of the cliff. Had I been yanked off my feet and the sled had landed upright, I wondered what would have happened. The cliff edge was not far away. Would the sled have dragged me into the void? A fall would have been fatal. The scariest part was that no one ever climbed there. I would have simply ceased to exist.

Deciding not to stay around and keep fighting, I stood up, righted my sled, and made my way to the edge of the chute to Squirrel Point. The surface was scoured and hard, making it easy from the crampons to bite in, but the slope was so steep I had to hold my sled below me. It was impossible to keep it behind me as it would have knocked me down and dragged me off the cliff.

The surface of Squirrel Hill was like rock. My axe bounced off the surface. Should I slip or be yanked off my feet by the sled, I wouldn't be able to stop. A mistake here, by myself, would be fatal.

"No problem. You can do this. So what if the wind keeps throwing rocks at your back?" I roared in my best drill sergeant tone.

"Focus on the positive! Visualize success. See yourself taking each step with confidence," I repeated in my mind.

Concentrating on stumbling or slipping would, I knew, cause me to do just that. Whatever I focused on would happen. The more fearful I became, the more energy I wasted. The only way to make it down was to keep repeating my mantra.

"You can do it. One step at a time."

I wrapped the sled line around my left hand to add extra shock absorption. My right hand held the ice axe, ready for a fall. I wanted to keep the sled under control. After a few minutes of down climbing, my left arm was on fire. There was no way I could hold onto the sled for the whole descent. I had to let the line slide through my hand. The individual bumps of the nylon rippled through my thick gloves. I didn't want to melt my glove by letting the line slide too quickly. I only had a few moments of strength left. Finally, the weight came onto my pack and the sled stopped.

As I stood there, I realized holding the line all the way down was impossible. After a few tentative steps, the sled jerked at my pack too much, causing me to stumble. The situation was dangerous. If my hand failed, I'd have no grip in the event of a fall. There was no way to hold onto the rope long enough to make the descent. Letting the sled tug on my pack was hurting my back.

The only way to do it was to hold onto the line, walk as far down as I could, and then switch hands between the sled and the ice axe. That way I could keep moving and not completely burn up either arm. When I stopped, I laid the line across my thigh to buffer the sled as it swung like a pendulum back and forth in the wind.

Switching hands took time but it worked. As I reached the first flat area, a barrage of small rocks clattered onto my helmet for a quarter of a minute. It was loud enough to give me a headache. I hadn't anticipated needing earplugs.

"I love it!" I yelled.

As I began the second part of the descent, I saw climbers below me on Motorcycle Hill making the turn to come up the chute to Squirrel Point. My eyes bugged out for a moment in astonishment. "Were they insane?" I thought to myself. The danger from the wind had to be obvious. They could see that from 11k camp, yet they were still climbing. Now this team coming up would join me in craziness.

In ten minutes, I met up with the first pair of climbers.

"Hello! It's incredibly windy up high!" I yelled at the top of my voice to the man nearest to me.

We were nearly face-to-face, as there was little room to pass one another. The climber looked at me in confusion, as though he didn't understand. I repeated my warning. I couldn't see his eyes through his goggles, so I wasn't sure if he understood. Then, I figured it out.

"Do you speak English?"

"Non, parlez-vous français?"

I swore under my breath. For all the time I spent studying French in high school, I remembered little. All useful phrases escaped me. I pointed up the hill and yelled, "Très mal!"

"Ah, oui, merci. We move," he yelled back.

It only took a moment for me to realize that this team was not turning back. They saw how dangerous the conditions were. Here I was again, hoping to keep someone out of danger. Perhaps they'd been through far worse and to them this was a walk in the park.

"Okay. Bon chance, mon ami!"

The climber nodded and let me pass. Another blast of rocks flew by. The French climber held his hands up to protect his face. Then he waved the others forward. I wondered if they would make it past Windy Corner. Though I knew none of them, I wished them the best. They were heading into brutal conditions.

I reached the small plateau at the top of Motorcycle Hill after struggling another fifteen minutes. Once I was out of the wind the difference was stunning. Only a few hundred feet further up, rocks flew by. Only a light breeze moved through 11k camp. I now knew why people chose to stop here, despite the searing heat.

Looking down, I saw that 11k camp had tripled in size since I'd left nearly a week before. Two teams of five climbers were fifty feet below me. Walking back to the cornice, I peered down the cliff I had almost blown off. The view was magnificent. Thousands of feet below me was Peters Basin. I wondered if anyone had ever been to the bottom. Turning toward camp, I encountered the first climbing team.

"Hello there! Are you planning on going up to Squirrel Point?"

"Maybe. We'll have to decide."

"The wind is blowing ice and rocks off the cliff. It's pretty rough up there."

"Well, good to know. We saw the flying snow and wondered."

"The French team is going up anyway. They must enjoy having rock sprayed in their faces."

"Thanks. There's a crevasse that's opened up at the bottom of the hill."

"Things have changed since I came through."

"Sure have. It's best to step over the open part. That way you know what you're in for."

"Thank you. I appreciate the beta."

"Not a problem. Good luck!"

We nodded to each other and I continued climbing down. I stepped to the right to let the two teams pass. If I lost control of my sled, I didn't want it to knock anyone down. Some of the climbers looked at me and smiled. Others didn't look up. I wondered if they were having a good time, focused and overloaded—or were they afraid? I didn't want to break their concentration, so I just moved past.

At the bottom of the slope, the crevasse waited for me. I had walked over it several times and had had no idea it was there. Thinking back to how the climber died in the book *Minus 148°*, I thought how easily I could have been entombed. Shaking my head, I hopped over the blue-black slash and yanked my sled over. The gap wasn't big enough to eat my sled, but I didn't want to test my luck.

Walking into camp, I looked for my cache marker. In a few minutes, I found it under an additional two feet of snow. The whole time I was at 14k camp, I wondered if someone had dug up my cache. Why would anyone dig it up? I grew up in a big city, so such thoughts are always on my mind. It is a cardinal mountaineering sin to damage or steal someone's cache, but there's always a first time.

Digging up the cache was tough. I had failed to place a wand in the exact center, and the hard ice from my stomping on it made shoveling a challenge. After ten minutes of concerted digging, my snowshoes and cache bags saw daylight. My cache was undisturbed and well protected.

I debated continuing down the mountain. I had plenty of supplies to keep going, but then I thought it would be better to take it easy, to enjoy the time, as my climb was over. It was 3:00 p.m. I wanted to leave but I knew I needed the rest.

After stomping out a flat spot in the snow, I pitched my tent. I wasn't going to make the same mistake that I did when I made camp here the week before. When the spot was smoothed, flattened, and leveled I walked around, chatting with people and relaxing.

About an hour after I finished setting up camp, four climbers descended Motorcycle Hill. Two of them were the Romanians.

"Hi, Ovidiu! I'm glad to see you two made it down safely. It was exciting up there!"

"Yes, thank you. We had some company coming down the mountain."

"Nothing wrong with a friendly ranger escort after a wind storm."

Smiling at the four of them, I thanked the two park service climbers for being with them.

"Just thought we'd help," one of them said.

At 6:00 p.m., the air cooled down and camp became tolerable. Should I decide to attempt Denali again, I planned to spend as little time at 11k camp as possible. The heat was crushing. I wanted to build a snow wall to hide from the sun but was too tired.

Thoughts of Felix crossed my mind. How long would it take for the weather to clear so he could move up to high camp? As long as he felt good, he had an excellent chance of making it with my supplies. I smiled, knowing my rations might make it possible for someone else to reach the summit even if I didn't.

The sound of white gas stoves and the scent of ramen filled the air. Every so often, a subtle waft of barbecue meat filled my nostrils. I salivated at the thought of the pulled pork sandwich waiting for me in Talkeetna.

As the sun plunged behind the mountains, shadows crept up Motorcycle Hill. I sat watching the procession, disappointed at having to abort my climb. I kept telling myself that returning alive without frostbite was more important.

I kept thinking about how warm I'd felt while being blasted on Windy Corner. Had I tapped into some unknown heat source inside of me? Was there a way to stave off hypothermia and frostbite in lethal conditions?

Thoughts of success, failure, and motivation coursed through my mind. In the dusky light I waited for sleep. The sounds of camp died down as other climbers slipped inside their tents. I wondered if the park service lent a tent to the Romanians for the night.

≈

If you alter or even abandon your mission, see if you can find some way to help others benefit from your experience. Often you'll learn more from failures than successes.

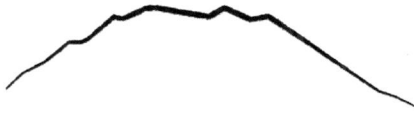

CHAPTER 17
May 23, 2016
Blind hike from 11k to base camp

When I woke up at 11k camp, the weather on the lower glacier was snowy and windy. It should make for a fun trip back to base camp, I predicted. Several teams were already climbing up Motorcycle Hill at 8:00 a.m., trying to get the jump on the roasting sun in the afternoon.

I had learned the hard way that climbing in the afternoon was excruciating. After 1:00 p.m., the sun was so intense that strenuous effort made me nauseous. Others didn't appear to mind climbing in clothes that soaked with sweat from the beating sun. I concluded that I needed to train in sunny, difficult conditions in the future. I didn't find being in freezing, sub-zero temperatures in a blinding whiteout too difficult. I had learned to deal with the cold end of the thermometer. Unless I planned to move to Antarctica or the Arctic permanently, however, I needed to become more adaptable.

I remained at 11k camp for a time and enjoyed the sight of the sun cresting over Squirrel Hill. I knew the glacier would heat up quickly, so I wanted to drop into the cool whiteout conditions below. The first teams climbing up from below were draped in snow. Although 11k camp was a broiler, it was safely above the unsettled weather on the lower part of the mountain. Every camp on Denali has its advantages and problems.

As I began hiking out of 11k camp, I passed the Romanians and asked them how they were doing.

"We are well and excited to be leaving," Ovidiu told me.

"How about you?" I asked Dor Geta.

"I'm glad I made it to the top, but am excited to be heading down now," she said.

Her perfect English blew me away. When I had last seen them on the mountain, Dor Geta couldn't utter a single word. And now, in calm conditions, she spoke polished English, with a slight accent.

"Do you have any cold injuries after losing your tent?" I asked.

Ovidiu took his worn, grimy glove off and showed me his waxy white thumb. It was enlarged to twice the normal size. I grimaced at the sight and offered my commiserations.

"Oh no, it's not that bad. This will heal easily. It happened from holding my ice axe," he said.

"I thought you had insulation on the top of the axe."

"Yes, I do. But there wasn't enough on there for me to hold it properly, so my thumb rested against metal for the entire time."

"So it was virtually unavoidable?"

"Yes, I'm afraid so."

"I have to congratulate you both. For reaching the summit in stormy conditions in only eight days, losing your tent, and only coming down with these tiny sleds is incredible."

"Thank you very much. I'm sorry you didn't make it to the top."

"That's okay. I didn't want to be trapped in seventy mile-per-hour winds. Plus, there wasn't enough time on my permit to wait out the weather."

"Good. This mountain is dangerous. It is better to stay alive and come back next season."

"That it is. How did you come up with so little gear?"

"We lost a lot higher up. But we did an acclimation climb on Orizaba before we came. That enabled us to make it to high camp in only eight days."

"Oh, my gosh, no wonder you could move so quickly. You were ready to go to the top almost immediately. The down suits probably make bad-weather travel easier."

"Yes, they do. At least we can handle severe wind without frostbite."

"Incredible. I have to commend you."

"Thank you."

"I'm sure I'll see you on the way down to base camp. I'll let you get on with your business."

I shook hands with both of them. It was incredible to see how little they had brought and yet had still managed to survive. They returned to breaking their camp down as I headed down the hill.

In only ten minutes of walking, I found myself in rolling clouds. The weather changed from stable and relatively warm to a complete whiteout in only two hundred yards of walking. Soon I was enveloped in icy fog and trying to find my way on an invisible trail. This section of Denali seemed to have consistently crummy weather.

As I made my way down the hill, I encountered several teams making their way up to 11k camp. One of the climbers was a soloist like myself. I couldn't believe my eyes, thinking that I was the only one crazy enough to tackle this mountain alone. We chatted for only a moment, as the wind snatched our words away before they reached each other's ears. He looked like he was struggling to make the last few hundreds of yards to camp, like I did.

"Do you know how much farther camp 11k is from here?" he asked dejectedly.

"You're almost there. I had the same experience a week ago, barely able to walk into camp. You'll come out of this whiteout and into camp in a few hundred yards. I know how you feel—it was the same for me a week ago."

"Did you make the summit?"

"No. The weather was bad and my permit would run out before I got a chance. I'm leaving with everyone else."

"Sorry to hear that. I'm pretty tired and just want to make camp. Good luck!" he said.

"Good luck to you, too. I hope things work out better for you."

We both nodded and smiled at each other through the blowing snow. As I was generating no heat walking downhill, I stopped and put on my light down jacket. When I looked back up the hill, he had already disappeared into the fog and horizontal snow. I stooped to tie a third knotted rope across the belly of my sled, significantly increasing the drag and preventing the orange tub from running me over during the descent.

It had taken me nearly an hour and a half to ascend this hill a week ago. Now, I reached the base of it in a mere half hour. Moving downhill into thicker atmosphere made walking fast and easy. Once I reached the bottom near my cache I untied all three drag cords. I didn't want to work any harder dragging my sled downhill than was absolutely necessary.

A constant stream of uphill climbers packed the trail, simplifying navigation. The clouds thinned as I went lower and in just a few minutes I located my cache. Even though I didn't need any of the food I had buried there, I was obligated to remove everything from the mountain. I was disappointed that I hadn't made the summit and I couldn't suppress the thought of removing the wands tagged with my permit and just abandoning the extra five pounds of supplies. No one would know the abandoned bags of food were mine as there were no identifying marks. It would have been easy to walk away, no one any the wiser. The snow would eventually melt in the summer, of course, revealing the cache. A few enterprising ravens and songbirds would have a feast. It was possible that the winter snows would bury the whole mess later in the year. Or it might become a mess that a park ranger would have to clean up.

Defeat and dejection make irresponsibility easier to justify. Nonetheless, I felt guilty at having such a thought, even in passing. Leaving a mess behind me, defiling a beautiful mountain with garbage, would bother me forever.

I wondered how many others ditched their supplies to escape the mountain. Other Denali expedition authors wrote of surviving off abandoned caches. Those same authors had left some in previous years. Others lucked out by finding someone else's supplies.

My internal debate only lasted thirty seconds, yet it felt like a half hour while standing in a constant storm at this altitude. There was no way I would leave trash on the mountain, just as I had not left garbage in Antarctica. I didn't want to be the one slob to trash an otherwise pristine environment. The struggle of temptation seemed to be universal, no matter where I was on the planet, or what condition I was in. Fatigue and defeat always intensified the struggle between the primitive, lazy self and the upstanding, conscious self.

It took significant effort to chisel through the hardened layers of ice to reach my cache. In the eleven days I had been away the snow I had packed down had turned to solid ice. While digging out my supplies, I guessed it would have been secure through the summer. Now I understood how it was possible for supplies to last multiple seasons on Denali.

I dragged the bag out of the four-foot deep pit and squashed it onto my sled. I wanted to keep moving down the mountain. I had seven more miles to walk in the soft snow.

By the time I reached Ski Hill, I was below the clouds. The afternoon sun beat down on me. Even though I traveled downhill, I couldn't believe how hot I was becoming. It was like being back at 11k camp. I stopped for an hour. No amount of removing clothes and drinking water brought me relief from the intense solar radiation. The snow was also slushy, increasing the chance of falling into a crevasse.

While I rested, the Polish team caught up with me. As they had lost their tent and gear, they traveled quickly. I shared a few snacks with them, as I suspected they were out of supplies.

I enjoyed watching them walk down to 7.9k camp, then out onto the expansive flat glacier. Soon they were a pair of colorful green and yellow ants in a gigantic landscape.

Once the heat subsided at 5:00 p.m., I resumed my journey. Now I saw how steep the two-tiered Ski Hill was. It hadn't been easy to ascent: without heel elevators on my snowshoes my calves had burned. I swore not to return to Denali without elevator snowshoes. It was too brutal and too slow without them.

When I first traveled through 7.9k camp, there were no other climbers. Now it was a bustling camp with dozens of colorful tents and it had morphed into quite an outpost.

At 6:00 p.m. I passed by a South Korean team making their way across the glacier. I couldn't believe my eyes. None of them wore snowshoes or skis. Only some of the men and women amongst them wore crampons. Most of them looked dejected and worn out. More than once, I saw one stumble, their unsupported feet punching into the partly slushy snow.

They had traveled across the glacier in the searing midday heat. Only the lead climber on each rope team looked up to acknowledge me. I stepped out their way. It looked as though each five-person rope team was on a forced march. Not joyful at all.

My steps were slow and plodding until the air cooled down at 8:00 p.m. Without a breeze, it took hours for the air to cool, even though it was surrounded by rock and ice. In the distance, I saw climbers making their way up Heartbreak Hill, on their way to base camp. All were moving as slowly as me.

When I finally reached the bottom of the slope leading to base camp, I stopped to relish the experience. Although I didn't summit, I wanted to enjoy the little time I had left in the Alaska Range.

As I rested, I heard the distant but powerful sound of flowing water. I realized I was listening to the subtle, snow-muffled flowing of an underground river under the glacier. I never imagined the water would flow with an audible sound. Perhaps there was a large fissure in the ice, letting the noise through. The sound unnerved me. It meant that somewhere nearby there might be a huge open hole down to this underground torrent. If I or someone else fell into it, it would mean certain death.

Should I return to Denali and attempt another solo climb, I would have to prepare to travel during the night and cool morning hours. But perhaps there were just too many hidden dangers lurking beneath the glacier for a single climber.

I arrived at base camp at 11:00 p.m., tired but happy. I was done. I found a comfortable spot, pitched my tent, and made dinner. While I was eating, several more teams dribbled in. It seemed this was an exodus. At least thirty tents dotted the upper slopes of the glacier.

I finished my favorite freeze-dried meal of spaghetti and meat sauce under the midnight sun. Even as I wriggled into my sleeping bag I heard more teams arriving and pitching camp. The distant sound of cascading avalanches lulled me into a fatigued sleep.

~

Managing your physical and emotional self is difficult after a defeat, even if it was unavoidable. Enjoy the walk back. You never know when or if you will return.

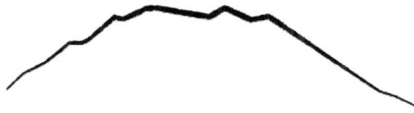

Chapter 18
May 24, 2016
Returning to civilization

I endured a recurring dream all night of being stuck in a snow cave on Denali Pass while 100 mph winds roared past. My mind was inside the book *Minus 148º*, where four climbers nearly perished while inside a snow cave. They were attempting to be the first team to climb Denali in the winter. My meager rations were nearly exhausted and there was no end in sight to the weather tearing across the mountain. Once my fuel for water ran out, I was forced to venture into winds that kept blowing me off my feet. Just as one overwhelming gust pushed me off the edge of the pass, I woke up.

My eyes were wide and I breathed deeply. It was the exact same feeling I had experienced when my sled became airborne near Squirrel Point. Being dragged toward the edge of the cliff fifty feet away by an out-of-control sled was an utter thrill. It caused my throat to dry and choke closed in an instant. Now, in my dream, I imagined an equivalent experience higher up the mountain.

The sounds of clattering tent poles and voices finally roused me from my stupor. It was already 7:30 a.m. Base camp buzzed with energy. Looking out, I saw dozens of people milling around, all keeping an eye on the crystal blue sky, awaiting aircraft. All at once, I remembered I needed to register with the flight crew. I had to sign up on the extraction list at 8:00 a.m.

I knew about the unwritten rule of disturbing the landing control crew out of hours.

"If you disturb us too early or late, you might find yourself on the bottom of a long list of people waiting to leave. Or, if you're particularly obnoxious, we might 'accidentally' lose your flight ticket."

This had all been said with a smile. But it had also been a not-so-subtle warning to treat the ground staff with courtesy. Having to say it at all suggested that there were many rude and irresponsible climbers. The staff clearly utilized creative techniques in tempering overbearing passengers.

I waited until one minute past eight before presenting myself at the ground control tent.

"Good morning, Lisa! Is it too early to disturb you for a flight out today?" I chimed.

Lisa flipped open the door flap.

"No, not at all. Thank you for waiting."

"Sure thing. I arrived at midnight and thought it best not to disturb you, lest I find myself at the bottom of the list."

She looked at me and smiled briefly. She shuffled through the papers to find my flight registration. It seemed that without it, I would be walking rather than flying home. I silently wondered what happened if a ticket was misplaced, but I refrained from asking. I didn't want to imply that they were disorganized.

She found my ticket and verified it. No disorganization here.

"Okay, I've got you on the list. Should the weather hold, I'll let you know which of the K2 planes you'll be on."

"There seems to be a mass of people here. Did everyone bail out at once?"

"Not quite. The weather has prevented anyone from flying for five days."

"Are you kidding? That's crazy."

"It does happen sometimes. Please gather by the landing strip at nine. There will be several waves of aircraft flying in and out."

I removed myself from the tent and returned to mine. I only had an hour to eat, pack, and prepare myself for the return flight. Fortunately the weather was stable and the sky was clear. The flags were motionless. My arrival at base camp had coincided with a stable flight window.

I didn't waste time tidying up. Instead, I jammed everything into my backpack and sled bag. I would sort it all out after returning to Talkeetna.

The crowd at the ice landing strip grew rapidly. There were more than fifty people milling around, each glancing toward the sky every few minutes.

Imperceptible at first, the drone of the first aircraft became steadily more audible. As a Talkeetna Air Taxi aircraft cleared the nearest mountain edge and made the turn toward Kahiltna glacier, a large avalanche broke loose above the camp. Everyone turned to look.

What seemed to be a small wave of dusty snow cascaded down the unnamed cliff face and slowly dissipated. The roar rippled across the narrow valley, reverberating and booming. Although the slide looked small, I knew better. It could have been a quarter of a mile wide. The perception of scale on Denali is distorted. The avalanche was a last reminder of the power and danger of the mountain I was leaving.

I thought about the pair of F-22 fighters that buzzed by 14k. They didn't touch off any avalanches that I heard, but the roar of their powerful engines could have. It was exciting to watch them. But with what just happened, I was mindful that aircraft fly-bys could trigger avalanches on a mountain.

Once the first aircraft touched down on the ice, another flew over the same mountain as the first. This time no more avalanches broke loose. A few minutes after the second Talkeetna Air Taxi single engine Otter landed, a third came into view. This pattern repeated again and again. All told, five Talkeetna Air Taxi and three K2 Aviation aircraft landed on the glacial runway in the span of half an hour.

Even as the second half of the airplane armada came in, climbers were already shuffling toward their designated aircraft. There were at least sixty climbers waiting for extraction. Based on the dejected look on their faces, many of them were demoralized. The strong winds that had forced me to abandon my attempt had affected dozens of teams.

One of the aircraft contained a few day tourists. They had flown up to the glacier with the initial wave of aircraft and now walked around taking pictures. They had two small children with them. When they attempted to walk up the glacier toward the crevasses the pilot intercepted them, warning them not to wander.

"There are crevasses everywhere on this glacier, especially on that hill. You could fall through and be killed before we could rescue you."

"Oh, I see," said one of visitors, clad in a pristine white down jacket. "I didn't think the camping area was dangerous."

"Holes have opened up in the middle of camp. We want you to return safely."

The visitors retreated with the pilot and continued taking photographs. Having seen the fissures on the far side of the hill, I knew the danger they could have been heading for. The crevasses on top of the hill could hide a small apartment building. An airplane could crash in there and no one would ever spot it.

After this minor drama, a pilot called out my name. I asked if it would be okay to sit in the co-pilot's seat. He agreed and guided me in. I gingerly stepped over the controls. Everyone donned their ear protection and the pilot powered up the aircraft.

In a few minutes, we skidded down the ice runway and became airborne. The glacier fell away as we rose up into the high reaches of the Alaska Range. I relished the views as we turned down the Kahiltna glacier. The return flight to Talkeetna only took half an hour. It seemed brief compared to the inbound flight two weeks ago.

≈

Having gratitude for an experience is what keeps the attitude positive, even when things didn't work out as planned.

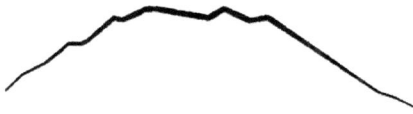

CHAPTER 19
Talkeetna

Talkeetna buzzed with tourists when I arrived. It was like returning to a completely different town. The one I had left was quiet, rainy, and empty. Now, people poured off buses and the train. The town had come alive while I was gone.

Over the remaining days of touring around Alaska, I had time to think about what had gone well and not-so-well on my climb. I stewed with doubt for some time about abandoning my summit attempt. Although the weather was poor at high camp when I left, I kept thinking that I had abandoned the climb too early. Reading the National Park Service (NPS) mountain blog changed my mind about that.

Around May 30, the park service reported that nearly half of all climbers descending from high camp reported some level of frostbite. Two climbers whom I had met while climbing were evacuated on May 30 with severe frostbite. One froze six toes, while the other froze eight fingers. They had ascended to high camp on May 17. They remained at high camp when I descended on May 22. Looking back, I can't believe they stuck it out at high camp that long. They had become trapped in what the park service dubbed Denali Storm Evans. This was the kind of wind blast that climbing rangers warn all teams about. The strong winds scoured off the 14k camp forecast on the park service white board.

Was it the most severe storm on Denali that season? Based on my reading of the park service blog, yes. However, it was certainly not the worst the mountain has ever seen. Not by a long shot. The book *Minus 148°* proves that.

A Czech climber whom I had seen earlier in my climb died on May 28 while skiing down the Messner Couloir, a steep couloir (a steep, narrow gully) that runs for a vertical mile. Presumably he hit an ice patch and tumbled out of control, falling 1,500 feet to his death. His teammates came down safely.

On the day before Felix reached the summit on June 1, only 19% of the parties attempting the climb had succeeded. The whole time I was on the upper mountain, few parties succeeded in reaching the summit, based on the park service blog.

Later in the season, one climber died from high-altitude pulmonary edema. The rescue party was unable to resuscitate him and he literally drowned in his own lung fluid. Another climber suffered from high-altitude cerebral edema but was successfully evacuated by the park staff.

Climbing Denali is a dangerous undertaking. In nearly every year since the early 1990s, one or more climbers have died attempting Denali, Foraker, and the surrounding glaciers.

By the end of the climbing seasons, a full 60% of climbers reached the summit. When I focus on that number, it's easy to become depressed. But then I look at the success rate while I was on the mountain and remind myself it was quite low.

My permit expired on June 1. I understand it was possible to change the date, but that would've put me in a marginal food situation. As the reports read, climbers were trapped at base camp for several days.

Even as I write this, I still debate whether I could have toughed it out. This is the difficulty of any abandoned attempt on an expedition. As a soloist, my margin for error is small. The goal is not to rely on others for food, fuel, and rescue if at all possible. Doing so would be irresponsible. Planning on pushing my climb to such a point that I would require assistance would be poor form. Others push to the edge and succeed, but the trade-off is an increase in the chance of injury or worse.

Even then, cautious climbers perish in the mountains. As an example, a well-known climber from British Columbia died in an avalanche in the University Range of Wrangell-St.Elias National Park in Alaska in 1999. Jim Haberl, author of *K2: Dreams and Reality*, had successfully climbed K2 and other mountains. In fact, his climbing partner died on K2 while they were descending. And Haberl was a cautious climber.

I have been asked countless times why I go on these expeditions. Why trek alone in Antarctica and Greenland, climb mountains, or travel to perilous places? The answer is as simple as it is complex—the satisfaction of being in nature and out of the city is immeasurable.

Travel in difficult conditions distills life down to two things: moving forward and surviving. There are many other human aspects involved, of course, such as having fun and taking photographs—but when I'm on these trips, all the noise of everyday life disappears. Emails, phone calls, texts, and the myriad other distractions of life vanish. It's like being an explorer or pioneer in the great age of exploration. If I don't take care of "it", whatever "it" is, no one else will.

There are classic quotes about why people climb mountains or explore polar regions. According to legend, when George Mallory was asked why he climbed Everest his reply was, "Because it's there." Whether he said it or not, the quote holds true for most adventurers. The thrill and satisfaction of the experience is worth the discomfort, suffering, and effort.

Another quote, attributed to several different people, is often referenced by adventurers: "For those who understand, no explanation is needed. For those who do not understand, no explanation is possible."

For someone who is seeking an answer to the why, this explanation offers nothing at all. I do not use it when speaking to audiences. The quote does nothing to further the explanation.

Instead, I offer this to those who think I'm crazy. Everyone has something in their life that makes sense to them. To some, this activity appears to be a senseless waste of time and money. We all pursue goals that make no sense to many others. My goal is to share the passion of my experiences through my speeches and books like this. They are made in the hope that the listener or reader will be inspired to pursue their own dream, whatever it might be.

To the reader, I ask you to consider this. Any activity, whether it be golfing, knitting, wood carving, or mountaineering, will always have detractors. People will say whatever you do is a waste of time. Don't listen to them.

Whatever your passion might be, transfer the joy and love of the experience in this book to yourself. Take it and use it to inspire what you do. Make your life the best you possibly can. Share your passion with others. You never know how you might positively impact someone else.

Personal Vision

After you've finished this book, you can put it on the shelf and call it an entertaining story. Or, you can use it as a learning experience.

Choose which you want to do.

To climb higher, turn the page and follow the exercises. Persevere to positively improve your life.

However you proceed, I hope you felt the experience in *Lost at Windy Corner*.

_____

_____

_____

_____

_____

_____

_____

_____

_____

_____

_____

_____

_____

_____

_____

_____

_____

What stories do you remember from *Lost at Windy Corner*? Think of a way to apply these experiences to your life to give you strength and resilience.

_____

_____

_____

_____

_____

_____

_____

_____

_____

_____

_____

_____

_____

_____

_____

What did you think of this process? Use these exercises to look at your life in a different way. Start with what you discover about yourself here to make an adjustment to how you do things.

_____

_____

_____

_____

_____

_____

_____

_____

_____

_____

_____

_____

_____

Using the stories in this book, think about the characteristics below. Using your own scale, write down how you perceive yourself now. Then, next to that number, write down how you would like to rate yourself.

- Grit _____

Courage _____

Attitude _____

Perseverance _____

Resilience _____

What goals do you have in each of the facets of life listed below? If you don't have any goals for these, think of some right now. When you're working toward something, it gives you a reason to wake up in the morning. All you have to do is make a little movement, however small, each day on your goals. Small steps take people to the top of the largest mountains.

When you write your goals down, they must be written in the positive present tense. By writing these down, your brain will treat them as something you need to do. Your subconscious will act on what you've written down to make these goals a reality.

Social/Volunteer _____

Family _____

Personal _____

Career _____

Fitness _____

List ten things you want to do in your life.

List ten places you want to visit in your life.

What stops you from doing these things? Are any of your destinations international? If so, visit the passport office and fill out an application. This small step only takes ten minutes but it can change the course of your life. Eliminate the petty excuses in your life. Stop dusting the baseboards. Walk to the foothills and take your first step up the mountain.

List the ways you will do this in your life. Be bold and dream big.

Find what is important to you. You may not want to climb Denali or ski alone to the South Pole, but there is something you want to do. Think big. It takes no effort to dream small as it does to dream big. How large can you dream?

You have the same twenty-four hours in the day as everyone else. When you look back at your life, make sure the view is the best you can make it. Sometimes you'll have to turn back before the summit. Be able to tell yourself in your heart that you did everything you could do to succeed. It takes grit to face down challenges.

When the next opportunity arises, take the one extra step beyond where you reached before. Have courage. This is your life. Have a positive attitude in the storms. Positivity can't make things happen but it does make things possible.

Thank you to my expedition sponsors:

Joel Attaway at 40 Below. Your booties are the best!

Kelly Gaffney
Nancy Takeda
Tim and Vicki Linsdau
Michael Cohen
Jantina Tuthill
Gerald and Linda Linsdau
Paul and Patricia Podell
Kenneth and Georgia Andrews
Joann Luu
Jackson Hole Juggernauts Roller Derby
William Leuallen
Joseph and Kiley Murdock

Other Books By The Author

50 Jackson Hole Photography Hotspots

This guide reveals the best Jackson Hole photography spots. Learn what locals and insiders know to find the most impressive and iconic photography locations in the United States. This is an excellent companion guide to the *Jackson Hole Hiking Guide*.

www.sastrugipress.com/books/50-jackson-hole-photography-hotspots/

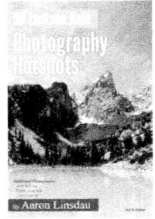

Adventure Expedition One
by Aaron Linsdau M.S. & Terry Williams, M.D.

Create, finance, enjoy, and return safely from your first expedition. Learn the techniques explorers use to achieve their goals and have a good time doing it. Acquire the skills, find the equipment, and learn the planning necessary to pull off an expedition.

www.sastrugipress.com/books/adventure-expedition-one/

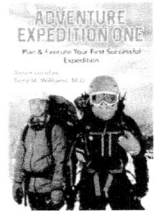

Antarctic Tears

Experience the honest story of solo polar exploration. This inspirational true book will make readers both cheer and cry. Coughing up blood and fighting skin-freezing temperatures were only a few of the perils Aaron Linsdau faced. Travel with him on a world-record expedition to the South Pole.

www.sastrugipress.com/books/antarctic-tears/

How to Keep Your Feet Warm in the Cold

Keep your feet warm in cold conditions on chilly adventures with techniques described in this book. Packed with dozens and dozens of ideas, learn how to avoid having cold feet ever again in your outdoor pursuits

www.sastrugipress.com/books/how-to-keep-your-feet-warm-in-the-cold/

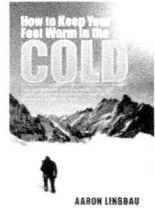

Jackson Hole Hiking Guide

Find the best hiking trails in Jackson Hole. You'll get maps, GPS coordinates, accurate routes, elevation info, highlights, and dangers. The guide includes easy, challenging, family-friendly, and ADA-accessible trails and hikes.

www.sastrugipress.com/books/jackson-hole-hiking-guide/

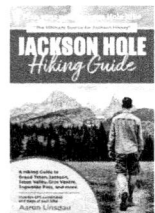

The Most Crucial Knots to Know

Knot tying is a skill everyone can use in daily life. This book shows how to tie over 40 of the most practical knots for virtually any situation. This guide will equip readers with skills that are useful, fun to learn, and will make you look like a confident pro.

www.sastrugipress.com/books/the-most-crucial-knots-to-know/

The Motivated Amateur's Guide to Winter Camping

Winter camping is one of the most satisfying ways to experience the wilderness. It is also the most challenging style of overnighting in the outdoors. Learn 100+ tips from a professional polar explorer on how to winter camp safely and be comfortable in the cold.

www.sastrugipress.com/books/the-motivated-amateurs-guide-to-winter-camping/

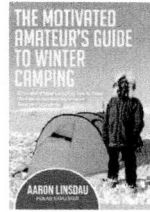

Two Friends and a Polar Bear
by Terry Williams, M.D. & Aaron Linsdau

This story of friendship is about two old friends who plan to ski across the Greenland Ice Cap along the Arctic Circle in hopes of becoming one of the oldest teams to succeed.

www.sastrugipress.com/books/two-friends-and-a-polar-bear/

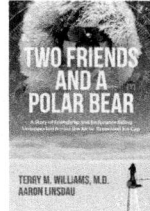

Use your smart device to scan the QR codes for website links.

Visit www.aaronlinsdau.com/subscribe/ and join his email list. Receive updates when he releases new books and shows. Book Aaron to speak at your next event.

Visit Sastrugi Press on the web at www.sastrugipress.com to purchase the above titles in bulk. They are available in print, e-book, or audiobook form.

About the Author

Aaron Linsdau is the second-only American to ski alone from the coast of Antarctica to the South Pole (730 miles / 1174 km). He set the world record for surviving the longest expedition ever for the Hercules Inlet to the South Pole route.

Aaron Linsdau at the South Pole.

Visit Aaron's YouTube channel: www.youtube.com/@alinsdau or scan the QR Code:

Other Sastrugi Press Books

50 Florida Wildlife Hotspots by Moose Henderson Ph.D.

This is a definitive guide to finding where to photograph wildlife in Florida. Follow the guidance of a professional wildlife photographer as he takes you to some of the best places to see wildlife in the Sunshine State.

www.sastrugipress.com/books/50-florida-wildlife-hotspots/

50 Wildlife Hotspots by Moose Henderson Ph.D.

Find out where to find animals and photograph them in Grand Teton National Park from a professional wildlife photographer. This unique guide shares the secret locations with the best chance at spotting wildlife.

www.sastrugipress.com/books/50-wildlife-hotspots/

Blood Justice by Tim W. James

Two brothers, one a preacher's son, the other an adopted would-be slave, set out in opposite directions to avenge their family's murder only to cross paths in pursuit of the killer.

www.sastrugipress.com/iron-spike-press/blood-justice/

Counterfeit Justice by Tim W. James

Preacher Roger Brinkman takes his crucifix and his Colt to fulfill a promise and help his lawman brother battle thieves, counterfeiters, and murderers in the Old West.

www.sastrugipress.com/iron-spike-press/counterfeit-justice/

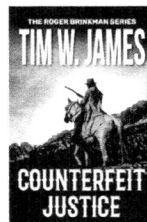

Journeys to the Edge by Randall Peeters, Ph.D.

What is it like to climb Mount Everest? Is it possible for you to actually make the ascent? It requires dreaming big and creating a personal vision to climb the mountains in your life. Randall Peeters shares his successes and failures and gives you some directly applicable guidelines on how you can create a vision for your life.

www.sastrugipress.com/books/journeys-to-the-edge/

Shake Yourself Free by Bob Millsap

Learn how to overcome difficult encounters with misfortune, tragedy, and loss. Emotional recovery is a journey requiring a mindset shift. Get this book now and take control of your life.

www.sastrugipress.com/books/shake-yourself-free/

So I Said by Gerry Spence

Venture into the mind of America's most famous lawyer. He shares his thoughts on hope, love, oppression, power, and life. Gain insight from a man who has fought overwhelming power and won from small-town Wyoming.

www.sastrugipress.com/books/so-i-said/

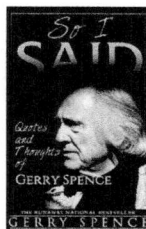

The Burqa Cave by Dean Petersen

Still haunted by Iraq, Tim Ross finds solace teaching high school in Wyoming. That is, until freshman David Jenkins reveals the murder of a lost local girl. Will Tim be able to overcome his demons to stop the murderer?

www.sastrugipress.com/books/the-burqa-cave/

The Diary of a Dude Wrangler by Struthers Burt

The dude ranch world of Struthers Burt was a romantic destination in the early twentieth century. He made Jackson Hole a tourist destination. These ranches were and still are popular destinations. Experience the origins of the modern old west.

www.sastrugipress.com/books/diary-of-a-dude-wrangler/

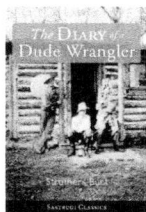

Printed in Dunstable, United Kingdom